Open and Nimble

DIRECTIONS IN DEVELOPMENT
Countries and Regions

Open and Nimble

Finding Stable Growth in Small Economies

Daniel Lederman and Justin T. Lesniak

Contents

Figures

Tables

Acknowledgments

This book was written by Daniel Lederman, a lead economist and deputy chief economist for the World Bank's Latin America and the Caribbean Region, and Justin T. Lesniak, a consultant in the World Bank's Office of the Chief Economist for Latin America and the Caribbean.

The authors gratefully acknowledge the early contributions of Jaime de Piniés to this book. The manuscript also benefited from research by Samuel Pienknagura and Diego Rojas (see Lederman, Pienknagura, and Rojas, "Latent Trade Diversification and Its Relevance for Macroeconomic Stability," 2015). Augusto de la Torre and Carlos Vegh, chief economists for the World Bank's Latin America and the Caribbean Region, provided insightful comments at various stages of this project.

The authors would also like to acknowledge the insightful comments of participants in the decision meeting held at the World Bank on September 21, 2016. We especially thank our meeting referees—Shahrokh Fardoust, Beata Javorcik, and David Rosenblatt—for their insightful comments. We are also grateful to have had the opportunity to present a conference edition of this work at a session of The Americas Conference Series, organized by the *Miami Herald*, and for comments received from participants there. Finally, we would like to thank two anonymous academic referees who reviewed the book.

We would like to acknowledge Ruth Delgado Flynn and Jacqueline Larrabure Rivero for the outstanding administrative support that they provided; Patricia Katayama, Aziz Gokdemir, and Jewel McFadden for their publishing support; Christelle Chapoy and the team at the *Miami Herald* for helping organize The Americas Conference event; and Michael Alwan for editing the book.

About the Authors

Daniel Lederman became lead economist and deputy chief economist for the Latin America and the Caribbean Region of the World Bank in May 2013. Previously, he served as lead trade economist in the World Bank's International Trade Department, senior economist in the Development Research Group, and senior economist and economist in the Office of the Chief Economist for Latin America and the Caribbean. Before joining the World Bank in 1995, he worked for the United Nations' Economic Commission for Latin America and the Caribbean.

An economist and political scientist by training, Lederman has published numerous books and articles on a broad set of issues related to economic development, including financial crises, crime, political economy of economic reforms, economic growth, innovation, international trade, and labor markets. His research has been published in the *American Economic Review, American Journal of Agricultural Economics, Journal of International Economics, Journal of Law and Economics, Journal of Development Economics, Economics and Politics,* and *Journal of International Business Studies,* among others. Books authored, coauthored, or edited by Lederman include *The Political Economy of Protection, Lessons from NAFTA* (also published in Spanish as *Lecciones del TLCAN), From Natural Resources to the Knowledge Economy* (also published in Spanish as *De los recursos naturales a la economía del conocimiento), Natural Resources: Neither Curse nor Destiny, Does What You Export Matter?, Latin American Entrepreneurs: Many Firms but Little Innovation,* and *Latin America and the Rising South.*

Lederman holds a B.A. in political science from Yale University and an M.A. and a Ph.D. from Johns Hopkins University's School of Advanced International Studies.

Justin Lesniak is a research analyst in the Office of the Chief Economist for Latin America and the Caribbean of the World Bank and has been with the office since 2015. In this role, Justin has contributed to important work, including the recent flagship report *Better Neighbors: Toward a Renewal of Economic Integration in Latin America,* as well as the writing of this book, *Open and Nimble: Finding*

Stable Growth in Small Economies. He is passionate about international development and particular issues related to international trade, urban economics, and regional economic inequality.

Justin holds B.A. degrees in economics and political science from the University of California, San Diego, and will be returning to pursue an M.A. in international affairs with a concentration in international economics and development at the school of Global Policy and Strategy starting in the fall of 2017.

Abbreviations

FDI   foreign direct investment
GDP   gross domestic product
HHI   Herfindahl-Hirschman Index
ILO   International Labor Organization
LAC   Latin America and the Caribbean
OECD   Organisation for Economic Co-operation and Development
OECS   Organisation of Eastern Caribbean States
PPP   purchasing power parity
SNA   System of National Accounts

CHAPTER 1

Introduction

Does the size of a country impact its economic development path? Are smaller countries at a disadvantage for achieving stable, long-run growth? It is not entirely clear, although there are good reasons to think size might matter. At an intuitive level, smaller countries would appear to have less resources to draw on (both in space and human capital terms) to create the industries and innovations necessary for sustaining long-run growth. In models of growth, economists often point to economies of scale, a factor closely related to size, as a key driver of growth. Many economic models also include economies of scale in knowledge generation, which would tie innovative capacity to country size. Given this context and the large number of small countries in the world today, the role of size in determining economic outcomes seems relatively underexplored. This book seeks to systematically explore the connections between size and economic outcomes and, ultimately, shed light on the role size might play in the process of economic development.

To illustrate the potential impact of size on the development process, consider the case of the Caribbean region. Over the past 40 years, it has seen average growth rates comparable to other developing regions.[1] However, from 1970 to 1990, the Caribbean significantly outperformed other developing regions, exceeding average annual growth (per capita) in the rest of Latin America by about 2 percent. Since 1990 the region has grown much more slowly, lagging the average annual growth rate in Latin America by about 0.5 percent. As is discussed later in this book, these patterns of growth in the Caribbean are at least in part due to volatility in the growth process of the Caribbean relative to that of the rest of Latin America—and, indeed, the rest of the world—conformed by larger economies.

Aside from the long-term volatility in growth rates, the Caribbean has been consistently among the world's leading regions in terms of foreign direct investment (FDI) inflows and international trade flows relative to gross domestic product (GDP), taking in significantly more FDI than the rest of Latin America. However, this openness to trade and FDI does not seem to be providing all of the expected growth benefits. In fact, Caribbean economies that exhibit the highest rates of FDI and international trade relative to GDP have not necessarily experienced higher growth rates. As mentioned, the Caribbean has had volatile GDP growth rates and has a high exposure to natural disasters as a region, yet savings rates remain low. Despite the clear need to save more for the future, Caribbean economies have had lower average savings rates than the rest of Latin America over the past 40 years. This book seeks to re-examine the economic growth potential of small economies with the aim of explaining these puzzling long-run economic outcomes in the Caribbean and other small economies.

One of the main conclusions of this book is that the Caribbean is not alone in facing these challenges. While some of the particulars of the above discussion are unique to the Caribbean, the general outline of the economic experience and challenges also describes in broad terms the economic path and challenges of small economies in Central America and other small states around the world. Although Caribbean countries may be a special case, given their status as extremely small islands in a region that faces recurrent natural disasters, the economic challenges that they face are not all that different from those faced by other small economies (albeit, ironically, they face them on a larger scale).

In a nutshell, then, this book argues that the size of an economy's labor force does have important implications for the process of development in a wide variety of countries. It studies the development challenges of small economies by systematically analyzing correlates of labor force size and, to a lesser extent, implications of the territorial space of nations. Following this introduction, the rest of the book is divided into five chapters.

The second chapter discusses basic economic characteristics of small economies. It begins by asking the question, what is a small economy? While this may seem obvious to some, there is no generally accepted answer in the literature. One must first decide the appropriate measure (land mass, population, or GDP are commonly used) and then decide upon how many "categories" of small there are, if any. Where necessary, this book adopts a broad definition of small (working age population less than the global median of 5.3 million). This reflects one of our main results: most of the relationships discussed in this book between size and macroeconomic variables are linear in nature, meaning that size may impact development even in countries not typically considered small.

The key finding of this chapter is that small economies are not necessarily limited in their development potential. GDP growth rates, as well as GDP per capita levels, do not seem to be correlated with size. However, while size does not necessarily hinder development outcomes, it may necessitate taking a different path toward development than that of large economies. Small economies may have different developmental challenges than large economies, which require different policy responses. Chapters 3 and 4 turn the discussion toward factors that make small economies unique in their development experience.

Chapter 3 documents a key characteristic of small economies: a relative lack of economies of scale. Economies of scale refer to the idea that there are efficiency gains in production as you increase the scale of production, and these are thought to be important for attaining long-run economic growth. While difficult to measure using international data, the chapter finds evidence of scale economies in several key areas, including export production, the ability to receive spillovers from FDI, and the cost of government.

In trade data, a lack of scale economies shows up in the high levels of specialization in export products and markets found among small economies. Small economies tend not to have the resources to compete effectively in international markets in a large number of export products at scale. Furthermore, trade with many partners likely requires covering certain fixed costs of market exploration and entry which are harder to pay for small economies. While high levels of specialization may help with competitiveness in international markets, they do not come without costs, as is discussed in chapter 4.

A second area where there is evidence of economies of scale is in the formation of backward linkages from FDI. In economic theory, FDI is particularly desirable because it allows for linkages between foreign and domestic firms so that best practices can be spread from more developed countries to less developed ones. However economic size seems to be positively related to the formation of backward linkages. A plausible explanation for this is that small economies just do not have firms in sufficient numbers or size to service the needs of the investing multinational companies.

Finally, small economies tend to spend relatively more on their governments as a share of GDP which is indicative of potential economies of scale in providing public services. Whether a country is large or small, there are certain public goods, such as transportation infrastructure and regulatory services, that must be provided to a minimum standard. The initial investment for small economies is costly given their relative lack of human capital resources.

Chapter 4 analyzes the implications of this lack of scale and resulting characteristics on economic outcomes, including high levels of economic volatility, relatively high costs of natural disasters, issues of fiscal management and debt, and low long-run savings. Small economies in Latin America and the Caribbean (LAC) and globally tend to face high levels of external economic volatility in the form of terms of trade volatility and GDP growth rate volatility. This external economic volatility is related to being a highly specialized economy—which, as chapter 3 discusses—is in turn related to being small. Adding to this economic volatility is the fact that small economies face relatively high costs of natural disasters as a share of GDP. The impact of these events is felt particularly strongly in LAC by the small island economies of the Caribbean.

With regard to fiscal management, smaller countries tend to spend more on providing public services due to a lack of economies of scale, which makes government more expensive as a share of GDP. While smallness seems related to higher government spending, smaller LAC economies face a unique problem: lower-than-expected government revenue generation. This is partly due to tax policies that might not be optimal for small economies, especially small island economies like those in the Caribbean. However, there also seems to be a regional factor at play, as LAC countries in general exhibit low government revenue generation. The result of these spending and revenue factors, combined with the high cost of natural disasters, is high levels of public debt in some small economies, and particularly in LAC. In LAC, countries in the Caribbean carry a large debt-to-GDP burden, likely due to their particularly acute vulnerability to natural disasters.

The above factors come together to create an important challenge to long-run growth in small economies: low long-run domestic savings rates. As just discussed, many small economies face high public debt burdens, limiting the ability of the public sector to increase savings. On the private sector side, the increased uncertainty of living in a small economy, resulting from high economic volatility and relatively higher disaster costs, may lead private agents to save less than would be optimal. Low savings rates are linked to lower investment, which in turn is linked to lower growth.

Chapter 5 highlights the fact that small economies have adapted to these economic challenges. One way in which small economies have adapted is by being more open. Smaller economies tend to be much more open, to both trade and investment, than larger economies, and evidence indicates this openness is beneficial for growth. Openness to trade provides a larger market for firms in small economies, potentially allowing them to achieve scale in more industries than they otherwise might. Openness to investment allows small economies to increase their investment levels and potentially offset some of the issues caused by low domestic savings rates.

A second feature of small economies is that they are incredibly nimble over time in terms of their export basket. Small economies typically have specialized export sectors in a given year, and this specialization is linked to higher volatility in both terms of trade and GDP growth. However, novel evidence presented in this book suggests that while small economies may not be able to produce many products contemporaneously, they have become adept at shifting the types of products they produce over time more quickly than large economies do. This nimbleness allows them to respond to the international market and may result in less economic volatility from terms of trade shocks than they might otherwise see.

Finally, the chapter discusses the issues of emigration and remittances in small economies. Small economies tend to have high levels of emigration, and this has led to high levels of remittances from migrants abroad. Remittances are in some sense an endogenous coping mechanism for small economies, as they tend to be countercyclical and responsive to natural disasters. However, they also have important implications for labor markets and labor market policy in small economies.

Finally, chapter 6 discusses possible policy solutions to the challenges of being a small economy generally and in the context of LAC. To be sure, certain aspects of being small, such as a lack of spillovers from FDI and relatively high costs of natural disasters, are difficult to resolve completely.

However, the impacts of most of the challenges noted above can be addressed via four policy objectives:

- Diversification of exports
- Deep regional integration efforts
- Tax reform
- Fiscal rules

Small countries are more open to trade, and therefore external volatility bites more than in larger economies. Nonetheless, the evidence suggests that diversification of exports across both products and export-market destinations can reduce terms of trade volatility. However, small economies may not be able to diversify in the traditional sense by making a greater variety of products. Therefore, it is helpful in such cases to think about diversification of exports over time, or nimbleness, a topic that is developed further in chapter 5. In addition, regional integration in a broader sense than just trade policies can help small economies by allowing, for example, for disaster risk pooling and cost pooling in the provision of public goods, and by stopping tax-code competition for foreign investment.

Chapter 6 also discusses fiscal policies. It argues that tax codes could be reformed in very small economies with the aim of reducing revenue-collection costs, thus raising potential revenues. In turn, such revenue gains could be literally saved for a rainy day (or used to pay back debt). To accomplish the latter objectives, the chapter and subsequent conclusions posit that small economies might be prime candidates for implementing fiscal rules with a strong pro-savings bias. This said, fiscal practices with a pro-savings bias might be politically difficult to implement without strict fiscal rules.

Many aspects of the challenges faced by small economies (relative to large economies) merit further research, and specific prescriptions go well beyond the scope of the present study. Our hope is that this book enhances our understanding of how economic size, represented by the size of the economically active population, affects key macroeconomic variables. With better understanding, we can hopefully pursue informed policy debates in small economies within Latin America and the Caribbean, as well as in any other context where limited supplies of labor affect the prospects for stable, long-term economic growth.

Note

1. Unless otherwise noted, the following 15 countries constitute the Caribbean here and throughout the book: Antigua and Barbuda, The Bahamas, Barbados, Belize, Dominica, Dominican Republic, Grenada, Guyana, Haiti, Jamaica, St. Kitts and Nevis, St. Lucia, St. Vincent and the Grenadines, Suriname, and Trinidad and Tobago. For information on other groupings used throughout this book, see the tables in appendix A.

CHAPTER 2

What Is a Small Economy?

What makes an economy small? And what, if anything, does economic size imply for a country's economic prospects? This chapter seeks to answer these questions as a foundation for the broader discussion in the rest of this book about how size is related to economic development outcomes. This chapter begins with a discussion of definitions and criteria used to classify countries as small, and then discusses, in the context of small countries in the Latin America and the Caribbean (LAC) region, what makes small economies different from each other. Specifically, the chapter classifies countries in LAC according to their product structure in exports. We use this classification throughout the rest of this book to better understand the role that differences in economic structure among small economies might play in determining economic outcomes. Finally, the chapter clarifies an important point: The size of a country *is not* correlated directly with that country having lower long-run growth rates, or lower levels of gross domestic product (GDP) per capita. However, as is discussed in the rest of the book, economic size may impact development indirectly and condition economic behavior in important ways.

What Is a "Small" Economy?

Before beginning a discussion of the impact of size on development and the challenges faced by small economies, it is necessary to briefly discuss what constitutes a small economy, a distinction not as clear as it might first appear. First, a choice must be made about the variable of interest in defining economic size. Three options emerge from the literature: GDP levels, population or labor force size, and land area.[1] Most often, when used in this book, economic size refers to labor force size (working age population), but results are also shown by income groupings in most figures. The role of limited land area, particularly in the context of small island states such as the Caribbean, is noted where appropriate and is particularly important in the discussion of natural disasters. While recognizing the value of analyzing all three elements of size listed above, we feel that labor force proxied by working age population provides the clearest overall measure of a country's economic size and best suits our analysis of the relationship between size and long-run development outcomes, given that it is a slow-moving demographic variable. The choice to emphasize labor force size is supported by the work of Crowards (2002), who defines small countries by considering all three of the aforementioned dimensions of size using cluster analysis techniques. He finds minimal differences between the countries identified as small by his method and traditional lists of small countries based solely on population size cutoffs.

The second issue that arises when talking about small economies is a discussion of thresholds and cutoff levels for what constitutes small in whichever indicator is used. Historically, population size has been used to determine whether or not a state is small, and the cutoff levels have been somewhat arbitrary, ranging from a population of less than 10 million (Streeten 1993) to 1.5 million (Commonwealth Secretariat / World Bank 2000).[2] Thresholds have generally decreased over time as the number of smaller states in the world has grown, hinting at their arbitrary nature, and many authors now attempt to make the distinction between small and micro states.[3] In our analysis, we split countries into different size groupings based on the quartiles of the global labor force distribution. We generally refer to countries in the lower 50 percent of the distribution, with working age population less than 5.3 million, as "small" (see appendix A for a discussion of how our cutoffs relate to LAC countries).[4] It is admittedly a fairly arbitrary choice, though this number and larger numbers in terms of population have been commonly used in previous literature (see Crowards 2002). The argument for choosing this number stems in part from one of the main results presented throughout the rest of the book, namely, that our chosen measure of economic size is almost in all cases (log) linearly correlated with the macroeconomic variables studied.[5] Such correlation implies that, while smaller states may face stronger versions of the common challenges discussed throughout this book, economic size also affects development in states not usually considered small.

Before discussing the implications of small economic size for economic outcomes, we consider the significant heterogeneity in such economies. In the next section, we focus on the role of heterogeneity in small LAC economies.

Differences in Economic Orientation among Small Economies in LAC

To study the role of heterogeneity among small economies, we look in particular at small LAC economies and variations in their economic structure as shown in export data. Some LAC countries are exporters of primary goods, while others specialize in services or manufactured goods. These differences in economic structure have potentially important impacts on how an economy functions and how it responds to economic shocks.

In a paper commissioned for this book, de Piniés, Varma, and Wacker (2015) distinguish Caribbean economies based on the composition of their export revenues. They define three types of economic "orientation": service oriented,

service and manufacturing oriented, and commodity-export oriented economies. They classify Caribbean economies as one of the three, depending on the
share of exports a country has in a given category of trade. Here, we follow the
spirit of their exercise and extend the classification scheme to other small
economies in Latin America. Figure 2.1 shows the composition of exports for
small LAC economies across the broad categories of services, manufactures,
and primary goods. From the figure, it is clear that the economies vary in composition of their exports, but most fit fairly neatly into one of the given categories.[6]
Going from left to right in figure 2.1, it is evident that many Caribbean islands
as well as Panama and Belize are service-oriented economies, at least by
exports. Countries in the region that primarily export primary goods include
Bolivia, Paraguay, and Uruguay in South America, as well as Guyana, Trinidad
and Tobago, and Suriname. El Salvador, Haiti, and Costa Rica have relatively
large manufacturing exports, while Honduras and Nicaragua exhibit a more
mixed export structure.

Although small economies face numerous common challenges, as discussed
throughout the rest of this book, grasping the important differences among them,

Figure 2.1 Export Value Decomposition for Small Economies in Latin America and the Caribbean, 2014

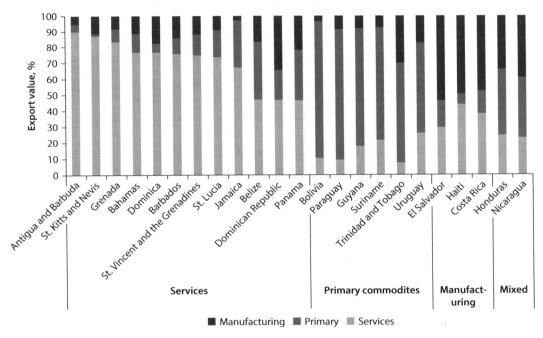

Source: Calculations based on a similar chart in de Piniés, Varma, and Wacker (2015, 3, figure 2), using trade data on goods and services from
UNCTAD stat trade matrices. We have updated their figure using more recent data and to include small Latin American countries outside
of the Caribbean.

Note: The figure shows the share of a country's total export value coming from services, manufactures, or primary goods. Some data are estimates
or predictions (see UNCTAD Stat methodology). Trinidad and Tobago data on service trade are for 2011, the most recent year available. Primary
commodities (SITC 0 + 1 + 2 + 3 + 4 + 68) include food and live animals; beverages and tobacco; minerals, fuels, and lubricants; animal and
vegetable oils, fats, waxes; and metals. Manufactured goods (SITC 5 to 8, less 667 and 68) include manufactured goods, machinery and transport
equipment, and other miscellaneous manufactured articles.

such as the structural differences just discussed, may also be of importance for understanding economic outcomes. Consider figure 2.2, which shows the trend component of long-run per capita growth in small economies in LAC by subregion over the period 1970–2013. The figure displays clear heterogeneity in the region's economic growth trends, even though all are considered small economies by our labor force size definition discussed above. Commodity exporters, perhaps benefiting from rising commodity prices, have seen much higher rates of growth recently than in the past, while service-oriented economies have seen consistently declining growth since roughly the 1990s.

Table 2.1, reproduced here and in appendix A, summarizes the classification scheme for small LAC economies used throughout the rest of this book. The scheme helps clarify how different types of LAC economies experience the common challenges associated with being small. That is, as will become evident hereafter, economic size shapes the process of development, even among economies with notable structural differences.

Figure 2.2 Differing Long-Term Growth Trends in Small Economies in Latin America and the Caribbean, 1981–2013

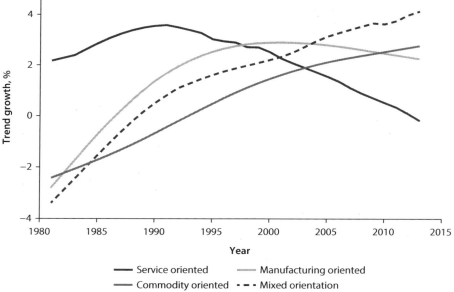

Sources: Calculations based on a similar chart in de Piniés, Varma, and Wacker (2015, 6, figure 7) using data from the World Development Indicators database. We updated their figure to include small Latin American countries outside of the Caribbean.

Note: The figure shows the trend growth rate of GDP per capita (in 2005 US$) for different groupings of LAC countries. First, annual growth rates of GDP per capita (in 2005 US$) are calculated for each small LAC economy. Then the Hodrik-Prescott filtering technique is applied to these series to isolate trend growth in each country in each year. This filtering produces the trend lines in the figure, which represent the median-trend growth of countries in each export grouping in a given year. Countries not included due to the fact that they do not report GDP per capita in all years: Haiti.

Table 2.1 Small Economies in Latin America and the Caribbean by Export Orientation, 2014

Service oriented	Commodity oriented	Manufacturing oriented	Mixed
Antigua and Barbuda	Guyana	Costa Rica	Honduras
Bahamas, The	Paraguay	El Salvador	Nicaragua
Barbados	Suriname	Haiti	
Belize	Trinidad and Tobago		
Dominica	Uruguay		
Dominican Republic	Bolivia		
Grenada			
Jamaica			
Panama			
St. Kitts and Nevis			
St. Lucia			
St. Vincent and the Grenadines			

Source: World Bank calculations based on data from UNCTAD Stat Trade Matrices.
Note: Categories are based on share of exports in services, manufactures, and primary goods in 2014. Countries are classified in a particular category if 45 percent or more of their export value was from goods or services within that category. Countries classified as mixed did not have a category with 45 percent of total export value.

Economic Size and Its Relationship with Growth Outcomes

Economic size has many implications for a country's development, which are discussed in the remainder of this book. That being said, it is important to first note that small size does not necessarily lead to lower growth rates or levels of development directly. However, small economic size does seem to affect a country's ability to achieve economies of scale (discussed in chapter 3), which is potentially important for the development process. Indeed, a key theme that runs throughout this book is that to the extent that economic size, or the size of an economy's labor force, is related to economic development, the relationship is indirect.

To facilitate comparing growth rates and levels of development (measured by GDP per capita) across economies of different sizes, we first illustrate the size distribution of labor forces worldwide. Figure 2.3 shows the median (or typical) labor force size of countries across several country and regional groupings. Many of the subsequent graphs presented in this book follow the same pattern as figure 2.3: we report the median values of the variable of interest for all country groups. The figure shows countries grouped as follows: (1) according to their economic size, measured by the number of potential workers or the working age population; (2) across different levels of development (following the World Bank's classification, which itself depends on each country's GDP per capita); (3) by region and subregion within LAC; and (4) by export orientation, as shown in table 2.1.[7] Note that the groupings (aside from income groupings) are listed from smallest to largest (by labor force size), from left to right. This order is maintained in subsequent graphs, so it will be easier to note when countries in these groupings differ significantly from the pattern we would expect them to follow based on size alone.

Open and Nimble • http://dx.doi.org/10.1596/978-1-4648-1042-8

Figure 2.3 LAC Labor Force Size in 2013

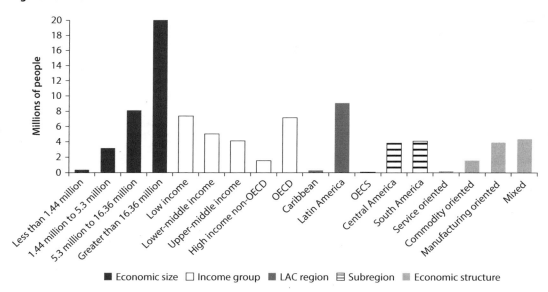

Source: Calculations based on data from the World Bank World Development Indicators database.
Note: Bars in the figure represent the median labor force value in 2013 among countries within each grouping. For the "greater than 16.36 million" labor force group, the median is 36.74 million people; the scale of the figure has been adjusted for better viewing of comparisons in the grouping. LAC countries not included due to lack of data: Dominica and St. Kitts and Nevis. OECS = Organisation of Eastern Caribbean States.

The distribution of labor force size across the income groupings depicted in figure 2.3 shows that high-income countries that are not official members of the Organisation for Economic Co-operation and Development (OECD) tend to have small labor force sizes. This is the first piece of evidence in this book indicating that small size per se does not seem to reduce an economy's long-term growth potential. If it did, we would not expect to see that the typical high-income country has a labor force below what is typical among low-income countries. It is also apparent that small economies in LAC range widely in size, from very small (Caribbean islands) to moderately small (small Central American and South American countries), making the region a good case study for understanding the potential impact of size. Finally, note that the manufacturing-oriented and mixed-orientation economies have group medians significantly larger than the service-oriented or commodity-export-oriented economies. It is argued in the rest of this book that in most of the relationships studied, this size discrepancy can help us understand the performance of these different groupings with regard to several macroeconomic variables.

Figures 2.4 and 2.5 present evidence that economic size is not directly related to levels of development or growth rates. Figure 2.4 shows the distribution of GDP per capita levels in 2013. From the distribution of GDP per capita purchasing power parity (PPP) across groups shown in figure 2.4, it does not appear that size negatively impacts development in a systematic way. In fact, countries in the Caribbean have similar levels of development to those in Latin America,

Figure 2.4 GDP per Capita PPP Levels in LAC, 2013

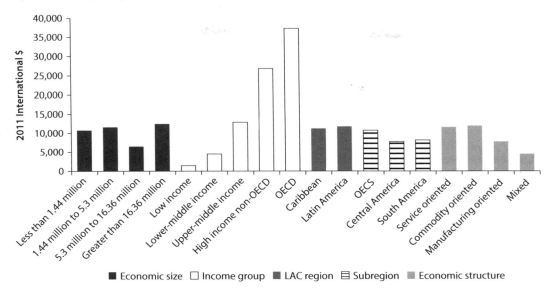

Legend: ■ Economic size □ Income group ■ LAC region ⊟ Subregion ■ Economic structure

Source: Calculations based on data from the World Bank World Development Indicators database.
Note: Bars represent the median value of GDP per capita PPP (2011 international dollars) among countries within each country group for 2013. LAC countries not included due to lack of data: Argentina. PPP = purchasing power parity.

which tend to be much bigger. Furthermore, the median member country in the Organisation of Eastern Caribbean States (OECS) has a higher level of development than small Central or South American economies with much bigger labor forces (see figure 2.3). These trends suggest, again, that a small labor force is not necessarily an impediment to achieving high levels of economic development.

Figure 2.5 highlights long-run GDP per capita growth rates from 1970 to 2013 across different country groupings. Again, there does not seem to be a consistent relationship between size and long-run economic growth, judging by the distribution of per capita growth across countries of varying labor force size. However, some interesting patterns emerge when comparing figures 2.4 and 2.5. High-income countries show a slightly higher long-run growth rate than the OECD, despite having lower GDP per capita PPP in 2013. Furthermore, the Caribbean region experienced significantly higher long-run growth rates than the rest of Latin America from 1970 to 2013; yet Caribbean GDP per capita roughly matched that of Latin America in 2013 for the median country. Finally, the service-oriented economies in LAC show very high per capita growth rates of almost 3 percent over the period 1970–2013; but this group trailed commodity-oriented countries in terms of GDP per capita PPP in 2013.

These cases highlight the role a country's growth path and volatility play in achieving high levels of development in the long run. As noted in chapter 1, Caribbean economies grew significantly faster than the rest of LAC from 1970 to 1990 and have underperformed since. Figure 2.2, discussed above, shows that

Figure 2.5 Long-Run Growth Rates in LAC, 1970–2013

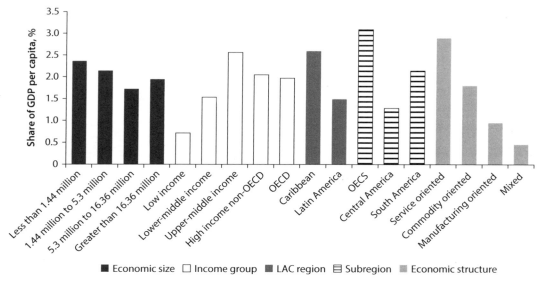

Source: Calculations based on data from World Bank World Development Indicators database.
Note: Bars are calculated by first taking the average growth of GDP per capita (in 2005 US$) over the period 1970–2013 for each country. The bar then represents the median value of that average among countries within each grouping. PPP = purchasing power parity.

service-oriented economies had significantly higher growth trends than LAC economies with different economic structures until the mid-1990s, but have done worse since about 2000. These growth episodes are not readily apparent from the long-run average growth rate data, but they are important in determining the development outcomes that countries achieve. Chapter 4 discusses in more detail the role of growth rate volatility as one channel through which size has implications for economic outcomes.

These descriptive statistics regarding size and country income are consistent with empirical findings in the economics literature. For example, Easterly and Kraay (2000) find that, after controlling for continental location and whether or not a country has oil, small countries tend to be richer than other states in per capita income. They also find no significant difference in growth rates between large and small states. De Piniés, Varma, and Wacker (2015) find no statistical relationship between labor force size and growth rates worldwide, but do find a correlation between labor force size and growth rate volatility (a relation hinted at in figures 2.4 and 2.5, expanded on in chapter 4). Alesina, Spolaore, and Wacziarg (2005) argue that one cannot analyze independently the effects of size and economic openness on growth. They find that while small size may have a negative impact on growth due to limited market size and opportunities for economies of scale, it is often coupled with high openness. Openness has a positive impact on growth by increasing market size and opportunities for exploiting economies of scale. In this way, any negative effects of small size on growth rates are counterbalanced by the positive effects of higher economic openness.

On the theoretical side, the literature on economic growth has struggled to reconcile the fact that there is no clear or direct empirical relationship between economic size and long-term growth. Most textbook models of economic growth include features of economies of scale. A good example of how theorists have handled the issue of economies of scale and its relationship with long-term economic growth is the work of Peretto and Valente (2015). These authors argue that economies of scale can be "neutralized" in theory so that the size of the economy does not directly determine the long-run level of GDP per capita. Their neutralizing mechanism shifts the economies-of-scale factor away from hypothetical firms and onto the number of firms in a given economy. This would occur, for example, when firms can be linked to international trade networks that fragment production chains into smaller pieces while the total global demand for a set of final goods is unchanged. As a result of global value chains, all economies, including small economies, will have only a few firms that achieve economies of scale. In turn, long-term growth is driven in all economies by the Schumpeterian dynamics of creative destruction. Peretto and Valente do not address the challenges of diversification and volatility, which are discussed later in this book. Nevertheless, their modeling approach would be consistent with the idea that small economies would tend to have fewer products in their production and export baskets.

In another recent paper, Ramondo, Rodriguez-Clare, and Saborio-Rodriguez (2016) address the issue of small size and economies of scale. They argue that when theories include knowledge generation as a driver of growth, it is often assumed that there are increasing returns to scale in knowledge generation, and the results seem to be inconsistent with global data (like ours) suggesting that small economies are just as likely as large ones to reach high-income status. In their view, the apparent disadvantages of being small are exaggerated in the existing theoretical literature, because it tends to assume that trade within countries is frictionless. This implies that trade between, say, New York and California in the United States would be costless because transportation costs within countries are close to zero. Thus, economies of scale would bite only when costly international transactions are involved, which would affect small economies disproportionately. Hence Ramondo, Rodriguez-Clare, and Saborio-Rodriguez (2016) introduce costs of trade within countries, in addition to costly trade across countries, in effect removing the disadvantage of being small. Either way, both the Peretto-Valente and the Ramondo et al. approaches predict that size is uncorrelated with long-term growth, and in both cases international trade plays a compensating role.

Although the research and evidence presented above do not find a direct impact of size on development, these recent theoretical models—as well as the results of Alesina, Spolaore and Wacziarg (2005)—highlight the fact that size may play an indirect role in the development process and that openness may be a key compensating factor. In fact, as will be seen when the data are discussed in chapter 5, one of the ways small economies have adapted to their size is by becoming more open and nimble. Despite this adaptation, the underlying issue of a lack of economies of scale in small economies brought up by these theorists is important for understanding the economics of small economies and is discussed further in the following chapter.

Notes

1. The appendix in Crowards (2002) contains a detailed review of literature from 1957 to 1999 and their criteria based on population, land, or GDP to classify small countries.

2. In fact, the Commonwealth Secretariat / World Bank report notes the arbitrary nature of its 1.5 million population classification: "In practice there is a continuum, with states larger than whatever threshold is chosen sharing some or all of the characteristics of smaller countries" (Commonwealth Secretariat / World Bank 2000).

3. Early literature identified the cutoff for "small" as between 5 and 10 million people. In the 1980s and 1990s it became fashionable to use 1 to 5 million people as a cutoff, and recently a common cutoff has been 1.5 million.

4. In the listing of small LAC countries, we include the Dominican Republic, Haiti, and Bolivia, even though these have working age populations greater than 5.3 million. We do this because the first two are often considered small in other research and all three countries have relatively small labor forces (less than 5 million workers in 2013).

5. All regression figures were also estimated nonparametrically with the LOWESS estimator. Cases where significant nonlinearity was found are discussed in the text. Results of nonparametric estimation for all regression figures included in this book are available upon request.

6. More formally, we use the following simple rule in assigning a country to a category: If a country has at least 45 percent of its trade in any one category, that is what we classify as the orientation of the economy. If no one sector has at least a 45 percent share of exports, then the economy is classified as mixed.

7. See country group tables in the appendix for a listing of all countries within each grouping used in the graphs throughout this book. Working age population cutoffs are quartiles from the global sample.

References

Alesina, Alberto, Enrico Spolaore, and Romain Wacziarg. 2005. "Trade, Growth, and the Size of Countries." In *Handbook of Economic Growth*, edited by P. Aghion and S. Durlauf. Amsterdam: North Holland.

Commonwealth Secretariat / World Bank. 2000. "Small States: Meeting Challenges in the Global Economy." Report of the Commonwealth Secretariat / World Bank Joint Task force on Small States. Washington, DC.

Crowards, Tim. 2002. "Defining the Category of Small States." *Journal of International Development* 14: 143–79.

De Piniés, Jaime, S. Varma, and K. Wacker. 2015. "Achieving Stable Growth through Diversification of Markets, Products and Services in the Caribbean: Stylized Facts." World Bank, Washington, DC.

Easterly, William, and Aart Kraay. 2000. "Small States, Small Problems? Income, Growth, and Volatility in Small States." *World Development* 28 (11): 2013–27.

Peretto, Pietro, and Simone Valente. 2015. "Growth on a Finite Planet: Resources, Technology, and Population in the Long Run." *Journal of Economic Growth* 20: 305–31.

Ramondo, Natalia, Andres Rodriguez-Clare, and Milagro Saborio-Rodriguez. 2016. "Trade, Domestic Frictions, and Scale Effects." *American Economic Review* 106 (10): 3159–84.

Streeten, Paul. 1993. "The Special Problems of Small Countries." *World Development* 21(2): 197–202.

CHAPTER 3

In Search of Scale Economies with International Data

Despite the fact that economic size is not correlated with levels of economic development or growth rates, it is potentially important with regard to one factor thought to be key in the development process: attaining economies of scale. Many economic models emphasize economies of scale as important for generating long-run economic growth and development. By definition, achieving economies of scale requires attainment of a certain size or scale in production, and thus it is logical to expect small economies to be less likely to attain economies of scale.

After briefly reviewing the economics literature on economies of scale, this chapter attempts to document the evidence of economies of scale (or lack thereof) in countries around the world using international data. The major caveat here is that evidence of scale economies is most often found when looking at micro or firm-level data and is difficult to detect precisely in higher-level data. That being said, there appears to be evidence of economies of scale in the patterns of international trade, in the provision of public services, and in the propensity of FDI to generate backward linkages. Each of these, and relevant economic literature, is discussed in turn. After presenting this evidence, chapter 4 turns to the potential implications of smallness for other economic outcomes.

Literature on Economies of Scale

Increasing returns to scale refers to the idea that output increases more than 1 for 1 with inputs for some industries or products. It is an important characteristic of many economic models explaining trade and growth outcomes. Krugman (1980) and others argue that economies of scale are essential for explaining observed patterns of trade among developed countries. He argues that there is a home market effect whereby countries with larger domestic markets may produce certain products even if they do not have comparative advantage in them; and this, along with transportation costs, can explain observed trade patterns and industry location behavior. Romer (1986) outlines a theory of endogenous long-run growth that is largely driven by economies of scale in knowledge generation, which he argues produce externalities that can lead to continuous long-term growth.

Despite these theoretical explanations of why economies of scale may be important in explaining growth and economic outcomes, it is difficult to determine if increasing returns to scale exist in practice and the impact they might be having. In terms of classical increasing returns, where increasing the scale of production in a firm lowers average costs, the evidence is mixed. Hall (1988) estimates returns to scale using a standard cost function and data on output and labor input in 26 U.S. industries and finds evidence consistent with increasing returns to scale. Caballero and Lyons (1989) build on the work of Hall by modifying his method of estimation to allow for the joint determinants of internal and external returns to scale. They find only 3 of 20 two-digit manufacturing industries in the United States show evidence of increasing returns to scale. However, there is strong evidence for the existence of external economies of scale (discussed below).[1] Burnside (1996) criticizes the approaches of Hall and Caballero and Lyons, arguing that their results are overly sensitive to sample and instrument choice and that they suppress essential firm heterogeneity by assuming that the returns to capital and labor are equal in all industries. Burnside estimates the production function again, allowing for different industries to experience different returns to capital and labor. He finds substantial heterogeneity, with only one industry showing evidence of increasing returns and most industries experiencing constant or even decreasing returns to scale. Hence, the literature does not appear to have reached a consensus on the nature or prevalence of internal increasing returns to scale. However, there is some evidence that electricity and energy generation is subject to economies of scale. Christensen and Greene (1976) estimate scale returns for U.S. electric power generation using plant-level data, finding that power generation is characterized by increasing returns to scale, at least at low levels of output. This is potentially important, given the key role of energy as an input for other industries.[2]

There is more evidence for external economies of scale or agglomeration economies. It is thought that firms in a particular industry often cluster together (agglomeration) because there are external economies of scale. In theory, agglomeration results in enhanced efficiency due to labor market pooling, knowledge spillovers between firms, and reduced transport costs for sending goods to market. Rosenthal and Strange (2004) review the literature on agglomeration economies and find that most studies support the idea that knowledge sharing, labor market pooling, and reduced transportation costs are all important sources of benefits for firms that locate close to one another. Hanson (2001) finds evidence that agglomeration creates positive externalities. Specifically, he finds that wages increase in the presence of more educated workers in the local labor force, and long-run industry growth is higher in locations with more industrial activity. Finally, Ellison, Glaeser, and Kerr (2010) analyze agglomeration patterns by looking at common characteristics of industries that tend to locate next to each other. They find evidence that the three channels discussed above—knowledge sharing, labor market pooling, and reduced transportation costs—are important in explaining agglomeration. However, they find that the most important factor determining whether firms located together is their need for natural resource endowments. Regardless of the form they take, economies of scale are thought to be an important component in generating growth, and it is worth investigating whether there is evidence of scale economies at the country level.

Economies of Scale in Trade Patterns

One area where evidence suggestive of scale effects can be found using international data is in trading patterns. One potential result of diseconomies of scale in small economies is specialization. In the context of increasing returns to scale, to effectively compete in international markets small economies need to achieve economies of scale in whatever product they are exporting. However, due to their small size, they are likely unable to gain scale economies in many products and are thus likely to exhibit highly specialized export sectors. To understand the nature and extent of specialization across economies of different sizes, this subsection looks at two well-established ways of measuring export concentration: the number of product lines a country exports each year, and a Herfindahl-Hirschman Index (HHI), which measures export revenue concentration across products. In turn, concentration in export destination markets for small economies is discussed. Finally, we present some rough estimates of production of goods with increasing returns to scale using export data, which support the idea that small economies are unable to gain comparative advantage in goods for which there is existing evidence of increasing returns to scale.

Concentration of Export Product Structure

The economics literature discusses export concentration in products mainly in the context of its relationship with development levels. According to the literature, export concentration is associated with lower levels of development and increased growth volatility. In their seminal paper, Imbs and Wacziarg (2003) find that countries' production patterns follow a U-shaped path with respect to development, meaning that countries tend to have a lower number of different industrial sectors at low levels of development and then diversify as they develop. Cadot, Carrère, and Strauss-Khan (2011) find that a country's degree of export concentration follows an inverted U-shaped pattern. This means that lower-income countries tend to have more concentrated export structures and produce fewer distinct products for export. Countries diversify as they develop up to a point, until a level of about 20,000 GDP per capita PPP, and then they begin to concentrate exports once more. Korren and Tenreyro (2007) find that as countries develop, they move from products in higher-volatility sectors to products in lower-volatility sectors. This seems to imply that, aside from highly developed countries, countries with highly concentrated export sectors are likely to experience some growth volatility, particularly if they are also highly open economies. We return to the relationship between growth volatility and specialization in chapter 4. In a departure from the current economic literature, which focuses mostly on links between development and specialization, we focus on the relationship between economic size and specialization for the remainder of this chapter.

Figure 3.1 shows the average number of exported product lines a country has across labor force size, income groupings, and regional groupings. It is clear from the distribution of the median number of export lines across labor force size that as countries become bigger in size, they tend to export a greater number of distinct products, with a large jump after the first quartile of the distribution and again between the third and fourth quartiles. The jump after reaching a working age population of 1.44 million likely reflects the influence of land mass as well as labor force on the number of products produced, since many countries with a labor force smaller than 1.44 million are small islands. The small land mass may limit the production of certain products or the total number of products. The low variety of exported products produced by the Caribbean islands and OECS countries in LAC relative to other LAC small countries reinforces that point. Again, when looking at the number

Figure 3.1 Number of Export Product Lines, 1995–2013

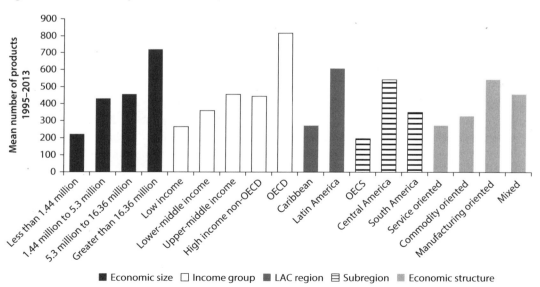

Sources: Calculations based on data from UN COMTRADE and the World Bank's Consolidated Data on International Trade in Services v8.8.
Note: Bars in the figure represent the median value of the average number of export lines from 1995 to 2013 among countries within each grouping. OECD = Organisation for Economic Co-operation and Development: OECS = Organisation of Eastern Caribbean States.

Open and Nimble • http://dx.doi.org/10.1596/978-1-4648-1042-8

of export lines that high-income non-OECD countries have, it is clear that producing a smaller number of products in a given year is not necessarily related to income levels. Finally, it appears that, broadly speaking, the distribution of the number of exported products by export structure follows a similar pattern to that predicted by the size of the economies in each structure grouping.

Figure 3.2 shows an alternative indicator of export concentration, namely, the Herfindahl-Hirschman Index (HHI) of export revenue concentration. A high HHI value indicates higher levels of export value concentration across product lines. We can see in figure 3.2 the same trend as in figure 3.1; small countries tend to have more concentrated exports, this time in terms of export value concentration. Again, there appear to be discrete drop-offs in concentration between the first and second quartiles and going from the third to the fourth quartiles. We also see that, in the context of LAC, small countries in Central America and the Caribbean are above the LAC average, with the

Figure 3.2 Herfindahl-Hirschman Index, 1995–2013

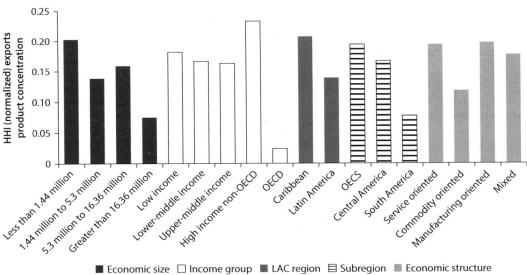

Sources: Calculations based on data from UN COMTRADE and the World Bank's Consolidated Data on International Trade in Services v8.8.
Note: The HHI values are calculated for each year and country individually using trade data in goods and services. They are calculated for each country and year as:

$$\Sigma \left(\frac{X_{ij}}{X_i} \right)^2$$

where X_{ij} represents the export value of product or service j from country i, and X_i represents total exports from country i. The data are then normalized to account for the fact that countries export different numbers of products. Then the average HHI value over the period 1995–2013 is calculated for each country. The bar then represents the median value of that series among countries within a given group.
HHI = Herfindahl-Hirschman Index; OECD = Organisation for Economic Co-operation and Development: OECS = Organisation of Eastern Caribbean States.

Caribbean showing significantly higher export value concentration. This is likely because of the significantly smaller labor force size of countries in the Caribbean grouping, as well as their status as islands with limited land. Also noteworthy is that OECD countries have significantly lower concentrations of export values than the other income groupings. Finally, we see that commodity-oriented small economies in Latin America and the Carribean appear to exhibit less export concentration than other small economies in the region, at least as measured by export product revenues.

Note that a plausible argument could be made that the connection we see in figures 3.1 and 3.2 is not about size per se. Rather, it could be the fact that small countries tend to be more open to trade that causes countries to specialize, perhaps due to competition effects from international markets or some other factor unrelated to size. Figures 3.3 and 3.4 document simple OLS regressions between size and openness, and between openness and the mean number of export lines. The relationship between size and openness is statistically significant and negative; small countries tend to be more open. The relation between openness and the mean number of exported products is also negative and statistically significant, indicating that more open economies tend to produce fewer products for export. Thus, figure 3.1 may be showing a relationship between size and the number of exported product lines that is driven not by size directly but by openness. It could be the case

Figure 3.3 Relationship between Size and Openness

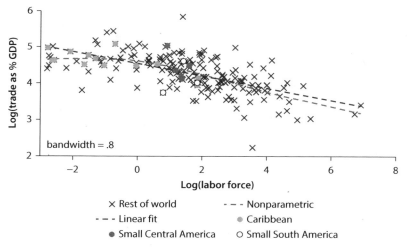

Source: Calculations based on data from World Bank World Development Indicators database.
Note: The straight fitted line in the figure represents the predicted values of the following linear regression:
Log(trade/GDP) = log(labor force) + error.
The coefficient on log(labor force) is −0.161 and is significant at the 1 percent level.
The curved fitted line was estimated with the nonparametric LOWESS estimator. The break point seen visually corresponds to a labor force size of roughly 417,000 people.

Figure 3.4 Relationship between Openness and Number of Export Lines

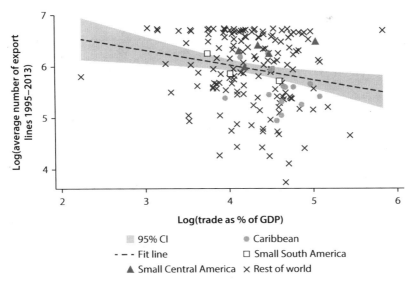

Sources: Calculations based on data from World Bank World Development Indicators database, UN COMTRADE, and the World Bank Consolidated Data on International Trade in Services v8.8.
Note: The straight fitted line in the figure represents the predicted values of the following linear regression:
Log(average # of export lines) = log(trade/GDP) + error.
The coefficient on log(trade/GDP) is −0.287 and is significant at the 1 percent level.
CI = confidence interval.

that small countries produce fewer distinct export lines not because they are small per se but because they are highly open to trade. This possibility for the number of export lines is explored further in figures 3.5 and 3.6, but the idea applies equally to the relationship observed with the HHI values.[3]

Note that figure 3.3 has not just a linear fit line but also a fit line estimated nonparametrically to account for potential nonlinearity in the data. One of the key findings of this book is that most of the relationships between size and other macroeconomic variables appear to be linear in nature, but figure 3.3 appears to be an exception. The nonlinear fit line rejoins the linear fit line at a point roughly equivalent to a labor force size of 417,100. This is likely because countries smaller than this size tend to be islands which are more heavily reliant on trade to supply goods for their population, given the limited land area available for production.

Figure 3.5 returns to the relationship between size, trade openness, and the number of export lines. The figure shows that, controlling for openness, size has the expected positive relationship with the average number of export lines: large economies export a greater variety of products than smaller ones. Figure 3.6, however, shows that, controlling for size, openness exhibits a positive, statistically significant relationship with the number of

Figure 3.5 Partial Correlation between Size and Number of Export Lines, Controlling for Openness

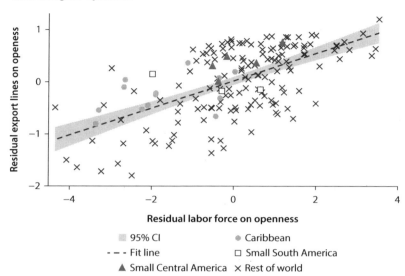

Sources: Calculations based on data from World Bank World Development Indicators database, UN COMTRADE, and World Bank Consolidated Data on International Trade in Services v8.8.
Note: Graph shows the fitted line of an ordinary least squares regression. It is calculated by first estimating the following two equations:
Log(average number of export lines) = log(openness) + error1; and log(labor force) = log(openness) + error2. Then the plot represents the regression of error1 on error2, which represents the relationship between labor force and export lines after controlling for openness. The relationship is positive with a coefficient of .259 that is significant at the 1 percent level.

export lines, rather than the expected negative one, if the above idea regarding international competition and specialization were true. That is, more open economies tend to produce more products, not fewer, when taking into account the role of size.

A potential reason for this is that open economies also tend to be more-developed countries.[4] As noted at the beginning of this subsection, the economics literature has documented the fact that countries typically become more diversified with higher levels of development, at least until they reach a very high GDP per capita threshold. When development and openness are controlled for, size retains its significant negative relationship with the average number of products produced; but when development and size are controlled for, the positive effect of openness loses its statistical significance. The conclusions discussed in this paragraph and the previous one hold analogously when looking at export concentration via the HHI index.[5] As development appears to be uncorrelated with size (figure 2.4), it seems likely that size is related to export concentration, independent of both openness and development.[6]

Figure 3.6 Partial Correlation between Openness and Number of Export Lines, Controlling for Size

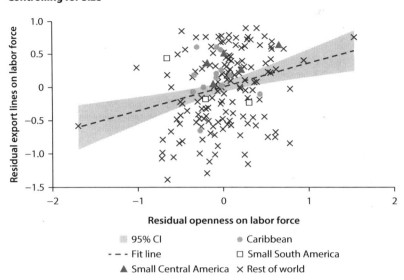

Sources: Calculations based on data from World Bank World Development Indicators database, UN COMTRADE, and World Bank Consolidated Data on International Trade in Services v8.8.
Note: Graph shows the fitted line of an ordinary least squares regression. It is calculated by first estimating the following two equations:
Log(average number of export lines) = log(labor force) + error1; and log(openness) = log(labor force) + error2
Then the plot represents the regression of error1 on error2, which represents the relationship between openness and average number of export lines after controlling for labor force size. The relationship is positive with a coefficient of .385 that is significant at the 1 percent level.

Specialization in Destination Markets

In addition to exhibiting concentration in export production structure, small economies also seem to exhibit concentration in terms of export markets. Although less discussed in the economics literature, concentration in export markets may play a role in the high levels of growth rate volatility that small countries experience, as discussed further in chapter 4.

Figure 3.7, which is analogous to figure 3.1, shows the median number of trading partners in each country grouping over the years 1995–2013. The distribution of trading partners over labor force size shows that smaller economies, despite being more open to trade as a share of GDP, tend to have fewer trading partners than larger economies. Looking at the number of trading partners by income grouping, we see that the median OECD country clearly has more trading partners than the median country of any other income grouping. Interestingly, countries in the Caribbean appear to trade with fewer partners than other LAC countries, including small economies in LAC. Finally, we see that the distribution of trading partners by export structure seems to roughly follow that predicted by the size of the economies; the smaller service-oriented and commodity-exporting economies

Figure 3.7 Number of Export Markets, 1995–2013

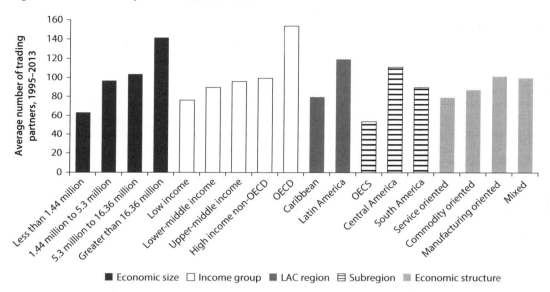

Sources: Calculations based on data from UN COMTRADE for trade in goods data and the World Bank's Consolidated Data on International Trade in Services v8.8.
Note: Bars are calculated first by taking the average number of trading partners per country over the period 1995–2013. The bar then represents the median value of that series for a given grouping of countries.

trade with fewer partners, while the larger manufacturing-oriented and mixed economies trade with more partners.

Figure 3.8, analogous to figure 3.2 above, shows the Herfindahl-Hirschman Index, calculated this time for concentration of export revenues across market destinations. When looking at the distribution across labor force groupings, the same pattern evident in figure 3.2 emerges in figure 3.8; size seems to be negatively correlated with the HHI for export markets. Looking at the distribution over income groups, we see a similar mixed relationship in figure 3.8 as we did in figure 3.2, with the OECD being significantly more diversified than the rest of the income groups. Looking at the grouping of small states in LAC, we see an important difference. While figure 3.2 showed countries in the OECS had by far the largest concentration of export values across products, figure 3.8 shows that Central America has significantly more concentrated export values by destination market. This likely reflects the historically, outsized role of the United States as a trade partner for the region.[7] Similarly, the U.S. role helps explains why the larger manufacturing-oriented and mixed economies in LAC show a larger concentration of export value by market than the smaller service-and commodity-oriented economies. Manufacturing-oriented and commodity-oriented economies are made up primarily of Central American countries, which conduct the bulk of their trade with the United States.

While the literature is scarce on the potential role of trading partner specialization in impacting growth, there is some evidence that having trading partners

Figure 3.8 Herfindahl-Hirschman Index Export Markets, 1995–2013

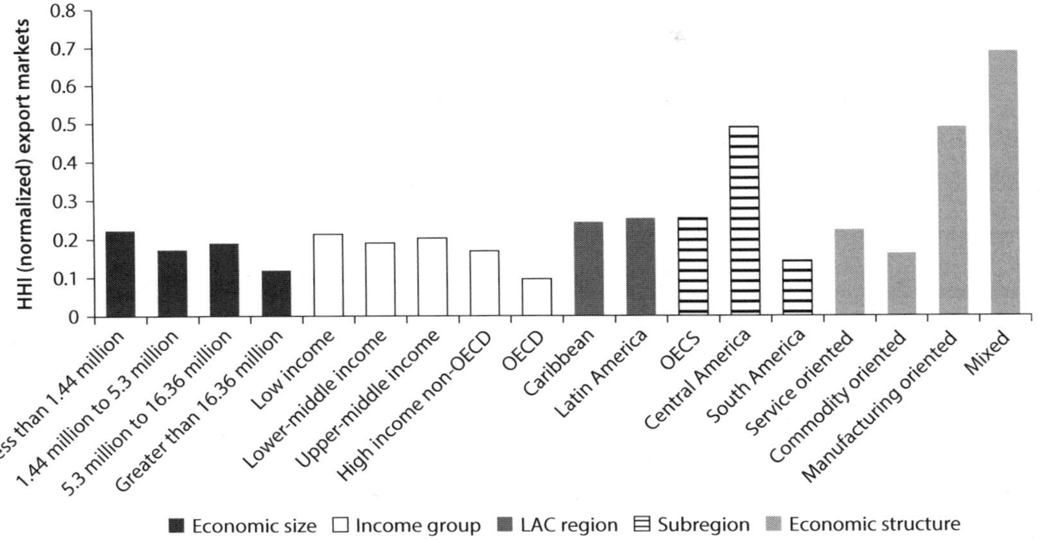

Sources: Calculations based on data from UN COMTRADE SITC1 for trade in goods data and the World Bank's Consolidated Data on International Trade in Services v8.8.

Note: HHI values are calculated for each year and country individually using trade data in goods and services, as follows:

$$\Sum \left(\frac{X_{ij}}{X_i} \right)^2$$

where X_{ij} represents the export value of trade from country i to country j, and X_i represents total exports from country i to the world. The data are then normalized to account for the fact that countries export to a different number of partners. Then the average HHI value over the period 1995–2013 is calculated for each country. The bar then represents the median value of that series among countries within a given group.

with certain characteristics matters for growth. Arora and Vamvakidis (2005) run growth regressions including standard controls (initial GDP, population, investment, human capital, inflation, trade openness), with per capita GDP and per capita GDP growth of trading partners weighted by their share of a country's exports. They find a strong effect (a 1 percent increase in a trading partner's growth implies as much as a 0.8 percent increase in domestic growth) that is robust to the inclusion of fixed effects. Additional discussion of the potential role of a country's trading partners in promoting growth can be found in a recent flagship report from the World Bank Office of the Chief Economist for LAC (Bown et al. 2017). The report tackles questions regarding the role of regional versus global integration in determining growth outcomes, as well as the role a country's neighborhood plays in determining its development prospects.

More directly addressing the role of trading partner diversification in promoting growth is the work of Onder and Yilmazkuday (2014). These authors take a network view of international trade and define three measures of how closely integrated countries are in the international trading network. The first is simply the share of total partners with which a country trades. The second measure takes into account the number of trading partners a country's partner has and the distance between countries in terms of trading partners. The third measure gives added weight to trade with important countries in the network. They find that all three of these measures of a country's centrality in the trading system correlate with growth when including country-fixed and time-fixed effects—as well as human capital, inflation, and exchange rate variables—in the regression. These authors also conduct a threshold analysis and find that countries can use their trading networks to compensate for low levels of financial depth, high inflation, and low levels of human capital. More will be said about the potential role of trading partner diversification in growth outcomes during the discussion of growth volatility in chapter 4.

Estimating Exports of Increasing Returns to Scale Products

Using trade data also allows one to directly estimate in a rudimentary way the relative production in an economy of goods that exhibit increasing returns to scale (assuming exported goods are representative of national production). If scale economies are present, then these goods should be exported more by relatively larger countries that can attain greater scale in their production. Figure 3.9 illustrates that this is indeed the case when looking at exported products. The figure shows the share of export values coming from industries estimated to have economies of scale across various country groupings, based on estimates by Antweiler and Trefler (2002).[8] These authors estimate scale returns at

Figure 3.9 Share of Exports in Increasing Returns to Scale Products, 1995–2013

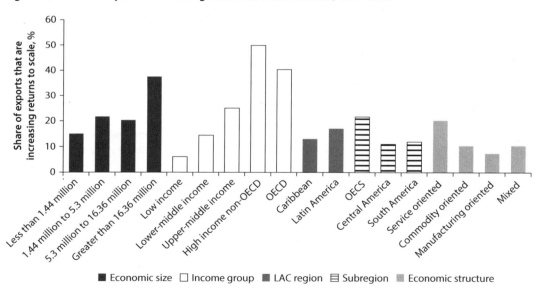

Sources: Calculations based on Antweiler and Treffler (2002) and goods trade data from UN COMTRADE.
Note: The figure represents the share of total exports going to industries estimated to have economies of scale by Antweiler and Treffler (2002). It is calculated by first finding the trade share of goods that exhibit increasing returns in each country in each year. The results are averaged by country, and the column then shows the median value for the 1995–2013 average trade share of goods with increasing returns to scale. Industries classified as having increasing returns to scale (using the United Nations' ISIC Rev 2 classification system) include livestock, forestry, coal mining, crude petroleum and natural gas, pharmaceuticals, petroleum refineries, petroleum and coal products, iron and steel basic industries, machinery and instruments, and electricity.

an aggregate industry level by using international trade data. They argue that trade data can be used to infer international price differences, and these price differences can be used without output data to estimate scale effects in a general equilibrium framework. It should be noted that the authors do not distinguish between classic internal returns to scale and potential industry agglomeration or external returns to scale.

The first thing to note in figure 3.9 is that small countries do not seem to be producing much in the way of goods with increasing returns to scale as a share of total exports. There was some theoretical evidence discussed in the previous chapter that high openness might play a compensating role in allowing small economies to achieve scale. It seems size still plays a substantial role in achieving scale, although one cannot say for sure whether or not small economies would be producing even less of these goods that exhibit increasing returns to scale if they were not so open to trade. Looking at the income distribution of trade shares in goods with increasing returns to scale, we see that the higher a country's income level, the more goods with increasing returns it tends to produce. Finally, as expected, small LAC economies have lower trade shares in goods with increasing returns to scale than the LAC average. The OECS and service-oriented countries account for a relatively high proportion of increasing returns goods trade. This result is driven by high levels of trade in increasing returns goods in St. Kitts and Nevis and Dominica.[9]

Scale Economies in Spillovers from Foreign Direct Investment?

A second area in which size seems to play a role and where there may be economies of scale present is in the formation of backward linkages using FDI. As small economies tend to be specialized, it may be the case that there are not domestic firms in sufficient number or at sufficient scale to connect with foreign firms. If this is the case, it would have important implications for the benefits of FDI in small economies, since this would imply that one of the key theoretical reasons why FDI is beneficial is less applicable to small economies.

According to the economics literature, there are three major types of FDI: horizontal, vertical, and platform. Horizontal or market-seeking FDI refers to companies that invest in another country at the same level of the value chain. Vertical or efficiency-seeking FDI refers to companies investing at different points in the value chain. Platform FDI is investment in another country geared toward exporting products to a third country. The small size of Caribbean economies would limit gains from horizontal FDI; therefore, most investment in the region is vertical FDI or platform FDI. Vertical FDI is hypothesized to provide positive growth spillovers in the country receiving the investment. Spillovers happen through transfers of technology from multinational companies to local suppliers (backward linkages), or through foreign companies supplying domestic companies more efficiently (forward linkages). Javorcik (2004) and Blalock and Gertler (2008) find evidence consistent with technology transfer and positive spillovers in Lithuania and Indonesia, respectively. In a large-scale meta-analysis of estimates on FDI spillovers in the economics literature, Havranek and Irsova (2011) find large, economically and statistically significant spillovers from backward linkages and statistically significant but economically small benefits from forward linkages. From this discussion, it seems that the type of FDI the Caribbean receives does not explain the lack of growth spillover effects in the region. Other potential explanations, include size and scale, need to be explored.

In a paper commissioned for this book, Antoine, de Piniés, and Sánchez-Martin (2015) analyze FDI and the potential for developing backward linkages globally and in the Caribbean in particular. Figure 3.10, a slightly modified figure from their paper, shows the relation between labor force size and backward linkages globally, demonstrating a strong positive correlation.

In this application, backward linkages are measured by the percentage of inputs of domestic origin used in production by a foreign firm. It may be the case that small size tends to limit access to backward linkages because small economies generally have fewer firms and are more specialized. Smaller economies also tend to serve more as export platforms, due to their limited domestic market opportunities.

Another potentially important factor in the development of backward linkages identified by Antoine, de Piniés, and Sánchez-Martin (2015) is the sector in which the investment is made. As will be seen in chapter 5, the Caribbean service-oriented economies have received more FDI than other countries in the region but have

Figure 3.10 Backward Linkages Increase with Size

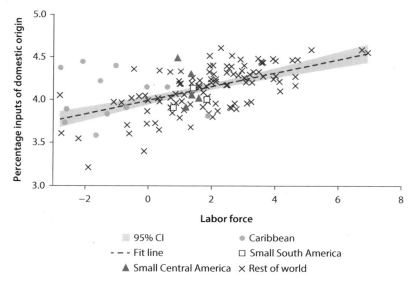

Sources: Calculations based on data from the World Bank Enterprise Surveys and World Bank World Development Indicators database.
Note: Graph shows fit line of the following linear regression: The country of Niger is not shown in the graph to improve the scale (but is included in the regression).
Log(percentage of inputs of domestic origin) = log(labor force) + error
The relationship is positive and statistically significant at the 1 percent level with a coefficient of .077.

Figure 3.11 Effects of Different Sectors on the Propensity to Form Backward Linkages

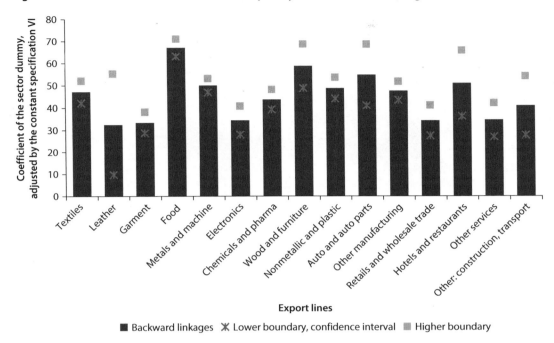

Source: Antoine, de Piniés, and Sánchez-Martin 2015.
Note: Bars represent the impact of being in a particular sector on the propensity to form backward linkages. The bars are coefficients of an ordinary least squares regression of sector of the firm on percentage of domestic inputs used in the product. Also included as controls are years of operation, percentage of skilled workers, use of quality certificates and foreign technology licenses, the percentage of foreign ownership of the firm, and the percentage of indirect exports (goods foreign companies produce and send to another company to export abroad). The bars represent the percentage of backward linkages of the average firm in a given sector.

not seen significantly elevated growth rates (see figure 2.4). Figure 3.11 shows estimates of the propensity of certain industrial sectors to develop backward linkages globally. The figure is taken from Antoine, de Piniés, and Sánchez-Martin (2015) and represents the results of their econometric model. The bars represent the propensity of a firm in a particular industry to form backward linkages when controlling for several other firm characteristics. It appears that traditional service sectors (food, hotels, and restaurants) do fairly well in promoting the development of backward linkages globally relative to other industries.

However, the authors note that Caribbean firms investing in service-oriented islands tend to have a very high use of foreign technologies, which the authors find is linked with a lower propensity for backward linkages. It may be the case that these economies do not have the skilled labor force necessary to develop backward linkages in more advanced services, but this is speculation.

It seems plausible that higher levels of skilled labor and education may be required to take full advantage of the technology spillovers and knowledge transfers that may be present with FDI. Figures 3.12 and 3.13 test this idea. Figure 3.12 shows the relation between size and FDI in a country, controlling for the average years of education of citizens over the age of 25.

Figure 3.12 Partial Correlation between Backward Linkages and Labor Force Size, Controlling for Average Years of Education Attained

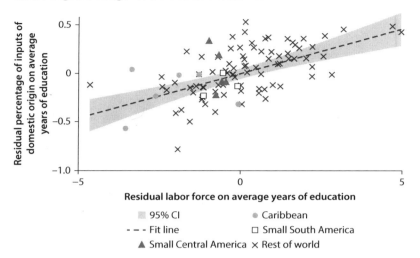

Sources: Calculations based on data from the Barro Lee Education Attainment Dataset, World Bank Enterprise Surveys, and World Bank World Development Indicators database.

Note: Graph shows the fit line of an ordinary least squares regression. It is calculated by first estimating the following two equations:

Log(percentage inputs of domestic origin) = log(average years of education) + error1

Log(labor force) = log(average years of education) + error2

Then the plot represents the regression of error1 on error2. This can be thought of as representing the relation between the percentage of domestic inputs a firm uses and the size of the labor force in a country, controlling for the average years of education. The relationship is positive with a coefficient of .092 and significant at the 1 percent level.

Size continues to have a positive and statistically significant relationship with our proxy for backward linkages. In contrast, figure 3.13 shows that education does not have a statistically significant relationship with the formation of backward linkages when controlling for labor force size.

Another factor that might indicate a country's ability to make use of technology or knowledge transfers from FDI is GDP per capita. When controlling for GDP per capita PPP, labor force size is positively related with backward linkages; but when controlling for labor force size, GDP per capita PPP is not related to backward linkages.[10] That is, when controlling for size, development levels do not seem to have any relationship with the level of backward linkages in an economy.

From this discussion, it is not entirely clear why size should be associated with lower levels of backward linkages in general or in the Caribbean specifically. In fact, the region's FDI inflows seem to be on focused on the exact industries that are typically prone to backward linkages worldwide. However, the evidence presented suggests that size does matter in the development of backward linkages. Specifically, one plausible explanation is that there just are not enough firms (or firms are not large enough) to supply multinationals. However, more research in this area is needed to say anything definitive.

Figure 3.13 Partial Correlation between Backward Linkages and Average Years of Education Attained, Controlling for Labor Force Size

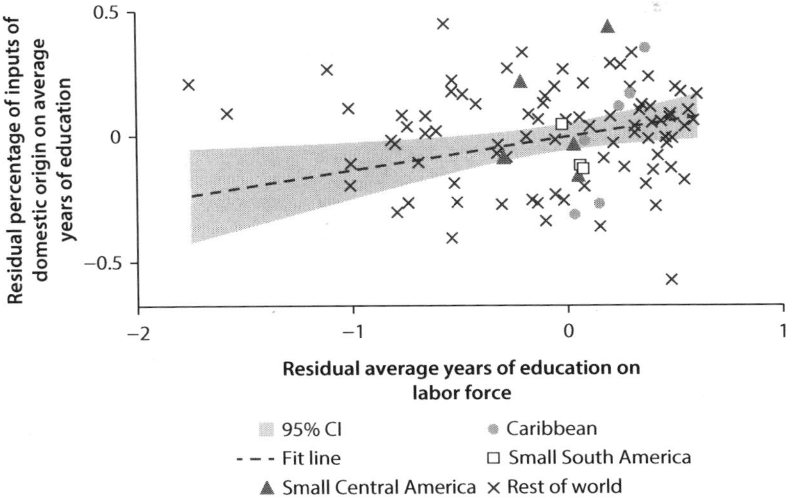

Sources: Calculations based on data from the Barro Lee Education Attainment Dataset, World Bank Enterprise Surveys, and World Bank World Development Indicators database.

Note: Graph shows the fit line of an ordinary least squares regression. It is calculated by first estimating the following two equations:

Log(percentage of inputs of domestic origin) = log(labor force) + error1
Log(average years of education) = log(labor force) + error2

Then the plot represents the regression of error1 on error2. This can be thought of as representing the relation between the percentage of domestic inputs a firm uses and the average years of education attained by workers in a country, controlling for the size of the labor force. The relationship is positive with a coefficient of .134, but it is not statistically significant.

Evidence of Scale Economies in Government

The final area where there appears to be some evidence of scale economies operating is government expenditure. Intuitively, this seems plausible as governments provide public services that have relatively high initial investments compared to the marginal costs of expansion and these fixed costs are spread across a small tax base in a small economy.

Figure 3.14 shows average, long-run government spending as a share of GDP across size, income, and region country groupings. From the distribution of government spending across labor force size, it appears that smaller countries tend to have higher ratios of government spending to GDP. It is also evident that higher-income countries tend to spend more on their governments, an effect independent of size, as discussed later in this section. Roughly the same pattern is evident when looking at LAC countries divided by economic orientation and when looking at the small countries within LAC.

Earlier research has noted that smaller economies tend to have higher government spending as a percentage of GDP. Alesina and Wacziarg (1998) use regressions (controlling for per capita income, urbanization, population density, and

Figure 3.14 Government Spending as a Share of GDP, 1990–2013

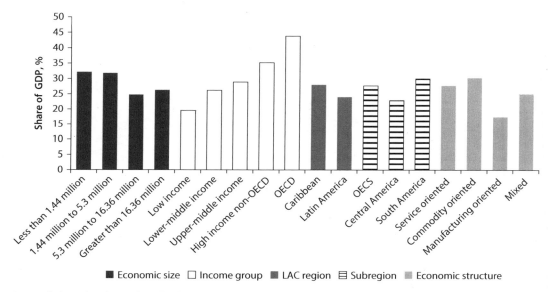

Source: Calculations based on April 2015 data from the IMF World Economic Outlook database.
Note: Bars represent the median of average government spending as a share of GDP from 1990 to 2013 among countries within each grouping.

region-specific effects) to show that a significant negative relation exists between government spending as a percentage of GDP and country population size. One explanation for this is that bigger countries achieve economies of scale in the provision of public services. There may be certain fixed costs of infrastructure construction and governance that lead small countries to spend more per capita on their governments than larger states. Favaro (2008) finds that, on average, small states spend 3.7 percentage points more of their GDP on producing public goods and services. This issue is conceivably of greater significance for small island states like those in the Caribbean; they must maintain costly airports, seaports, and other transportation infrastructure to be connected to the global economy and supply their population with goods they cannot produce.

As noted above, the distribution of government spending across income groups in figure 3.14 seems to show a positive relationship between income levels and government spending. Figures 3.15 and 3.16 show that both size and development are significantly related to government spending over GDP when controlling for each other. Figure 3.15 illustrates the impact of labor force size on government spending after controlling for level of development and shows the expected statistically significant negative correlation between the two. As countries get bigger, they seem to spend less as a percentage of GDP on their governments. However, figure 3.16 shows that when controlling for labor force size, development levels show a positive, statistically significant partial correlation with government spending. More developed countries tend to spend more on their governments. These two relationships are not inconsistent with each other,

Figure 3.15 Partial Correlation between Government Spending and Labor Force Size, Controlling for Level of GDP per Capita

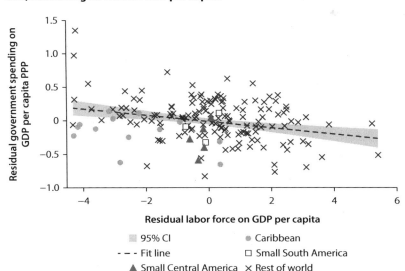

Sources: Calculations based on April 2015 data from IMF World Economic Outlook and World Bank World Development Indicators database.

Note: Graph shows the fit line of an ordinary least squares regression. It is calculated by first estimating the following two equations:

Log(government spending/GDP) = log(GDP per capita PPP) + error1

Log(labor force) = log(GDP per capita PPP) + error2

Then the plot represents the regression of error1 on error2. This represents the relationship between government/GDP and labor force size, controlling for differences in development levels. The relationship is negative and significant at the 1 percent level with a coefficient of −.047. PPP = purchasing power parity.

but note that they seem to play independent roles in terms of determining the size of government.

Notably, some research has found that more-open economies have larger governments. As small countries tend to be more open, it could be the case that high levels of openness contribute to the higher levels of government spending observed in figure 3.14. Rodrik (1998) finds a significant positive relationship between openness and the size of government when controlling for GDP per capita, urbanization, the dependency ratio in the population, whether or not a country is socialist or in the OECD, and regional effects. However, as noted earlier in this chapter, economic size is negatively related to openness; being small is associated with more openness to trade. Additionally, openness levels rise with development. These results are consistent with the idea that the observed positive association between openness and government spending as a share of GDP could come from small size and/or high development levels rather than openness per se. Rodrik tests this idea using population and land as measures of size, finding that openness retains a positive effect. We use labor force size to test the impact of openness.

Figure 3.16 Partial Correlation between Government Spending and GDP per Capita Levels, Controlling for Labor Force Size

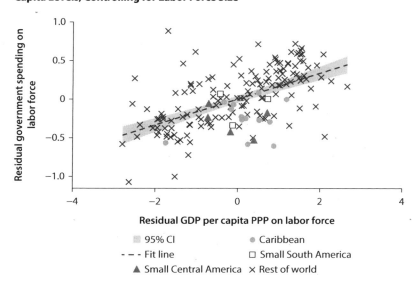

Sources: Calculations based on April 2015 data from IMF World Economic Outlook and World Bank World Development Indicators database.
Note: Graph shows the fit line of an ordinary least squares regression. It is calculated by first estimating the following two equations:
Log(government spending/GDP) = log(labor force) + error1
Log(GDP per capita PPP) = log(labor force) + error2
Then the plot represents the regression of error1 on error2. This represents the relationship between GDP per capita and government/GDP, controlling for labor force size. The relationship is positive and significant at the 1 percent level with a coefficient of .167. PPP = purchasing power parity.

Figure 3.17 shows that when taking into account the size of the labor force and levels of development, openness no longer has a significant positive association with government spending as a percentage of GDP, and in fact the estimated coefficient switches sign from positive to negative. Thus, at least in our data, it appears that any relation between openness and the government share of GDP occurs primarily through the size of the labor force and level of development, rather than any direct effect of openness on the size of government relative to GDP. This difference between Rodrik's results and ours based on different measures of size is interesting and could be explored in further research.

Government Revenues

In addition to the fact that small economies seem to face high costs of governance, economies in LAC face the additional challenge of relatively low government revenue generation. Figure 3.18 shows median average annual government revenue as a percentage of GDP from 1990 to 2013 for different country groupings. From the distribution of government revenue as a share of

Figure 3.17 Partial Correlation between Openness and Government Spending, Controlling for Labor Force Size and GDP per Capita Levels

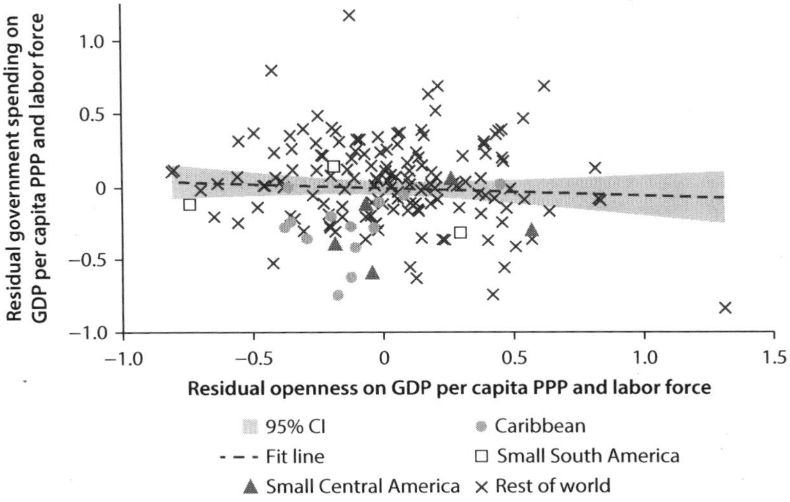

Source: Calculations based on April 2015 data from IMF World Economic Outlook and World Bank World Development Indicators database.

Note: The graph shows the fit line of an ordinary least squares regression. It is calculated by first estimating the following two equations:

Log(government spending/GDP) = log(GDP per capita PPP) + log(labor force) error1
Log(openness avg) = log(GDP per capita PPP) + log(labor force) + error2

Then the plot represents the regression of error1 on error2. This represents the relationships between openness and government spending when controlling for differing labor force and GDP per capita PPP levels. The relationship is negative with a coefficient of −.053, but **not significant**. PPP = purchasing power parity.

GDP over labor force size, it appears that small economies have relatively high revenue generation worldwide. Government revenue generation also seems to increase with income. However, small LAC economies exhibit relatively low public revenue generation compared to small economies worldwide. Revenue generation and issues of tax policy are discussed further in chapter 6. This low revenue generation, combined with the tendency of small economies to have larger governments, makes LAC's small economies particularly vulnerable to the problem of high debt levels in small economies, discussed in chapter 4.

What is clear from the discussion of this chapter is that there is substantial evidence suggestive of the idea that economies of scale are present in a number of important areas and they impact outcomes in small economies. Specifically, smaller countries tend to exhibit more specialization in their trading products/partners, have higher government spending relative to GDP, and have a lower propensity to form backward linkages with FDI. The implications of these findings are discussed further in the following chapter.

Figure 3.18 Government Revenue Generation, 1990–2013

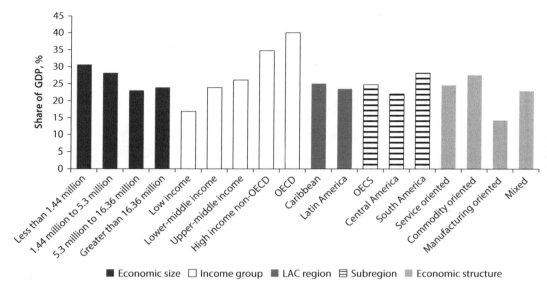

Source: Calculations based on data from IMF World Economic Outlook database April 2015.
Note: Bars represent the median value of average government revenue/GDP from 1990 to 2013 among countries within each grouping.

Notes

1. Caballero and Lyons (1990) also estimate returns to scale for manufacturing in Germany, France, the United Kingdom, and Belgium. They find only 3 of 13 industries exhibit internal returns to scale and none of those in more than two of the four countries studied. In contrast, evidence for external economies exists in all four countries.

2. Although we do not discuss scale in energy markets in detail here, the reader is referred to a recently published work by Beylis and Cunha, "Energy Pricing Policies for Inclusive Growth in Latin America and the Caribbean," from the Office of the Chief Economist for Latin America and the Caribbean, regarding the economics of electricity markets and energy generation in Latin America and the Caribbean.

3. Figure 3.2 shows that smaller countries tend to have higher HHI values. Regressing HHI values on log(openness) yields a positive relationship significant at the 5 percent level with a coefficient of .07. More-open countries tend to have higher HHI values. So the fact that smaller countries have high HHI values could be due to the fact that they are small or that they are highly open.

4. The regression of log(GDP per capita PPP) on log(trade openness) yields a coefficient of .101 on log(GDP per capita PPP) that is significant at the 1 percent level.

5. The partial correlation between labor force size and the HHI controlling for openness is negative, with a coefficient of −.232 that is statistically significant at the 1 percent level. Smaller countries tend to have larger HHI values. The partial correlation between openness and the HHI controlling for labor force size is negative, with a coefficient of −.319, significant at the 10 percent level. As with the number of products, this is the opposite sign on openness that we would expect if openness rather than size were driving concentration of export revenues.

Open and Nimble • http://dx.doi.org/10.1596/978-1-4648-1042-8

6. When controlling for development, the partial correlation between size and average number of exported products is .202 and is significant at the 1 percent level. When controlling for size, the partial correlation between development and average number of exported products is .323 and is significant at the 1 percent level. This holds for the HHI as well. When controlling for development, size regressed against the HHI has a coefficient of −.180. When controlling for size, development has a coefficient of −0.313. Both of these are significant at the 1 percent level.

7. In fact, for LAC the median value of 1995–2013 average share of exports to the United States is about 39.5 percent. The Central American median value is 68.7 percent. For Nicaragua and Honduras (which make up the mixed economic structure category), exports sent to the United States represent 82.7 percent and 83.0 percent of total exports, respectively. For Haiti, El Salvador, and Costa Rica (which make up the manufacturing-oriented category), exports sent to the United States represent 89.4 percent, 68.7 percent, and 41.5 percent of total exports, respectively.

8. We add electricity to the list of industries from Antweiler and Treffler, given the discussion above of economies of scale in electricity generation.

9. This result is driven by the fact that, over the period 1995–2013, trade in goods with increasing returns to scale for St. Kitts and Nevis averaged 70.6 percent of total exports and for Dominica it averaged 48.0 percent. In St. Kitts and Nevis this share mainly comes from trade in goods documented under ISIC rev2 code 383, "Manufacture of electrical machinery apparatus, appliances and supplies." In Dominica, the result was driven by large levels of trade in manufactured chemical products and other manufactured materials, both electrical and nonelectrical (ISIC codes 352, 382 and 383).

10. The partial correlation between log(labor force) and log(percentage inputs of domestic origin) is positive with a coefficient of .077 that is statistically significant at the 1 percent level. The partial correlation between log(GDP per capita PPP) and log(percentage inputs of domestic origin) is positive with a coefficient of .02 and is not statistically significant.

References

Alesina, Alberto, and Romain Wacziarg. 1998. "Openness, Country Size, and the Government." *Journal of Public Economics* 69 (3): 305–21.

Antoine, Kassia, Jaime de Piniés, and Miguel Eduardo Sánchez-Martin. 2015. "Measuring the Determinants of Backward Linkages from FDI in Developing Economies. Is It a Matter of Size?" Working Paper 7185, World Bank, Washington, DC.

Antweiler, Werner, and Daniel Trefler. 2002. "Increasing Returns and All That: A View from Trade." *American Economic Review* 92 (1): 93–119.

Arora, Vivek, and Athanasios Vamvakidis. 2005. "How Much Do Trading Partners Matter for Economic Growth?" *IMF Staff Papers* 52 (1): 24–40.

Beylis, Guillermo, and Barbara Cunha. 2017. *Energy Pricing Policies for Inclusive Growth in Latin America and the Caribbean.* Washington, D.C: World Bank.

Blalock, Garrick, and Paul Gertler. 2008. "Welfare Gains from Foreign Direct Investment through Technology Transfer to Local Suppliers." *Journal of International Economics* 74 (2): 402–21.

Bown, Chad, Daniel Lederman, Samuel Pienknagura, and Raymond Roberston. 2017. *Better Neighbors: Toward a Renewal of Economic Integration in Latin America.* Washington, DC: World Bank.

Burnside, Craig. 1996. "Production Function Regressions, Returns to Scale, and Externalities." *Journal of Monetary Economics* 37: 177–201.

Caballero, Ricardo, and Richard Lyons. 1989. "The Role of External Economies in U.S. Manufacturing." NBER Working Paper 3033, National Bureau of Economic Research, Cambridge, MA.

Caballero, Ricardo, and Richard Lyons. 1990. "Internal Versus External Economies in European Industry." *European Economic Review* 34: 805–30.

Cadot, Olivier, Celine Carrère, and Vanessa Strauss-Khan. 2011. "Export Diversification: What's Behind the Hump?" *Review of Economics and Statistics* 93 (2): 590–605.

Christensen, Laurits, and William H. Greene. 1976. "Economies of Scale in U.S. Electric Power Generation." *Journal of Political Economy* 84 (4): 655–76.

Ellison, Glen, Edward Glaeser, and William Kerr. 2010. "What Causes Industry Agglomeration? Evidence from Coagglomeration Patterns." *American Economic Review* 100 (3): 1195–1213.

Favaro, Edgardo, ed. 2008. *Small States, Smart Solutions: Improving Connectivity and Increasing the Efficiency of Public Services.* Washington, DC: World Bank.

Hall, Robert. 1988. "The Relation between Price and Marginal Cost in U.S. Industry." *Journal of Political Economy* 96 (5): 921–47.

Hanson, Gordon. 2007. "Emigration, Remittances, and Labor Force Participation in Mexico." INTAL-ITD Working Paper 28, Inter-American Development Bank, Washington, DC.

Havranek, Tomas, and Zuzana Irsova. 2011. "Estimating Vertical Spillovers from FDI: Why Results Vary and What the True Effect Is." *Journal of International Economics* 85 (2): 234–44.

Imbs, Jean, and Romain Wacziarg. 2003. "Stages of Diversification." *American Economic Review* 93 (1): 63–86.

Javorcik, B. S. 2004. "Does Foreign Direct Investment Increase the Productivity of Domestic Firms? In Search of Spillovers through Backward Linkages." *American Economic Review* 94 (3): 605–27.

Korren, Miklos, and Silvana Tenreyro. 2007. "Volatility and Development." *Quarterly Journal of Economics* 122 (1): 243–87.

Krugman, Paul. 1980. "Scale Economies, Product Differentiation, and the Pattern of Trade." *American Economic Review* 70 (5): 950–59.

Onder, Ali, and Hakan Yilmazkuday. 2014. "Trade Partner Diversification and Growth: How Trade Links Matter." Working Paper 192, Federal Reserve Bank of Dallas Globalization and Monetary Policy Institute.

Rodrik, Dani. 1998. "Why Do More Open Economies Have Bigger Governments?" *Journal of Political Economy* 106 (5): 997–1032.

Romer, Paul. 1986. "Increasing Returns and Long-Run Growth." *Journal of Political Economy* 94 (5): 1002–37.

Rosenthal, Stuart, and William Strange. 2004. "Evidence on the Natura and Sources of Agglomeration Economies." *Handbook of Regional and Urban Economics* 4: 2119–71.

CHAPTER 4

Implications for Economic Outcomes

The previous chapter established the importance of economies of scale in the development process and how their existence might impact small economies. Specifically, it was found that small economies tend to lack the ability to generate scale economies, and this manifests itself in several areas. These economies tend to have highly specialized export sectors, in terms of both products and destination markets, as well as high government spending relative to GDP and difficulty generating spillovers from FDI.

This chapter argues that these characteristics, combined with smallness, have contributed to several common challenges to development in these economies. These challenges are as follows: exposure to high economic volatility; high relative costs of natural disasters and fiscal management issues; and low long-term savings.

The first challenge, high external volatility, is relevant for small economies generally, as well as those in Latin America and the Caribbean (LAC). This issue stems in part from the specialized export sectors exhibited by small economies, as discussed in chapter 3. High terms of trade volatility, as well as export specialization, lead to the broader problem of GDP growth volatility in small economies, which has a negative impact on long-run GDP growth rates and development outcomes.

In addition to economic volatility, small states (particularly small island states) face higher relative costs from natural disasters. This not only results in high levels of disaster damages but may also negatively impact several economic variables, including consumption, savings, and the current account balance. Such impediments make achieving a stable growth path more difficult.

These issues, as well as the issue of scale raised in chapter 3, arguably contribute to issues of fiscal management in small economies. These economies face higher costs of governance due to an inability to achieve economies of scale in the provision of public goods and services, and small LAC economies also suffer from low levels of government revenue generation relative to small economies in the rest of the world. This, combined with the need to respond to volatile economic conditions and natural disasters, is a recipe for difficulties in fiscal management and high levels of public debt.

Finally, small economies exhibit low savings as a share of GDP relative to other countries in the world. There is some evidence that persistently low domestic savings lead to lower investment and lower potential long-run growth rates. This chapter discusses each of these challenges in turn.

External Economic Volatility

A lack of scale economies has contributed to small economies developing export sectors that are highly concentrated, both in the number of products they produce and the number of countries with which they trade. This specialization increases exposure to external volatility in small economies through two channels. The first is that exporting a limited number of products is associated with higher terms of trade volatility, which in turn is associated with higher growth rate volatility by affecting the value of a country's trade. Second, there is some evidence that having a limited number of trading partners is associated with increased growth volatility, by increasing the weight of partner demand shocks in the trade basket of the exporting country.

Terms of Trade Volatility

The role of terms of trade volatility in determining growth is well studied in the literature. Mendoza (1997) provides a formal growth model framework in which terms of trade volatility can impact growth. In his model, uncertainly impacts the savings and consumption patterns of individuals, and one cause of uncertainty in an economy is terms of trade volatility. In the model, increased variability in the return on exports (that is, increased terms of trade volatility) promotes a bias toward current consumption and away from savings if agents exhibit risk-averse behavior. Over time, lower savings rates lead to lower consumption and growth rates. Turnovsky and Chattopadhyay (2003) find that terms of trade volatility is negatively related to growth rates—more so in highly volatile economies. They estimate a model with three sources of volatility: fiscal policy, monetary policy, and terms of trade shocks. They find support for the idea that terms of trade matter for the equilibrium growth rate of countries, more so in countries that exhibit high growth rate volatility. Finally, Mendoza (1995) finds that terms of trade volatility is related to not just growth but also volatility in a country's growth rate. This volatility in growth rates may have a negative impact on long-run growth, as discussed in the next section of this chapter.

Figure 4.1 shows median terms of trade growth volatility from 1970 to 2013 by labor force size and income groupings, as well as for several groupings of LAC countries. Looking at the distribution of terms of trade volatility across labor force size, there does not appear to be a systematic relationship between size and terms of trade volatility. This is not surprising, as terms of trade volatility depends on the number of products a country produces and not size directly

Figure 4.1 Terms of Trade Growth Volatility, 1970–2013

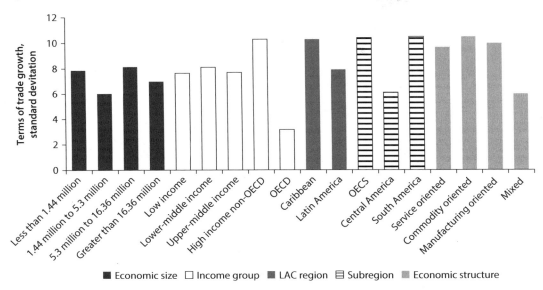

Source: Calculations based on data from Penn World Table 8.1 (Feenstra, Inklaar, and Timmer 2015).
Note: Terms of trade volatility was calculated using Penn World Tables price index data. First a ratio of the exports price index to the imports price index was calculated for each country and year for which data were available, from which the yearly change in terms of trade was computed for each country. Then the standard deviation of the annual change in terms of trade was computed for each country. Finally bars in the figure represent the median standard deviation of terms of trade growth among countries within each grouping.
LAC countries not included due to lack of data: Guyana, Haiti, and Nicaragua.

(as discussed below). It also seems unlikely that terms of trade volatility is systematically related to income levels, based on the distribution over income groupings.

Clearly, in the case of LAC, terms of trade volatility has been high in Latin America, particularly in the Caribbean. In terms of LAC small states, terms of trade volatility is particularly high in the OECS countries of the Caribbean and small states in South America. This finding—that terms of trade volatility is highest in the smallest and largest sets of the LAC small states—can be explained by the fact that the OECS and the small South American states produce the fewest number of products (see figure 3.1). The relationship between export specialization and terms of trade volatility is explored next.

One well-documented key determinant of terms of trade volatility is export concentration in products. For example, Lederman and Maloney (2012) find that, in fact, terms of trade volatility is positively related to export concentration, which they measure using the Herfindahl-Hirschman Index (HHI), and not necessarily with size directly. Others, such as Jansen (2004), also note this link between terms of trade volatility and export concentration, in this case measured as the number of products a country exports in a given year.

Figures 4.2 and 4.3 reinforce the point that terms of trade volatility is correlated with the number of export lines, a traditional measure of export diversification (discussed in chapter 3), rather than with size directly.

Figure 4.2 Partial Correlation between Terms of Trade Volatility and Number of Export Lines, Controlling for Labor Force

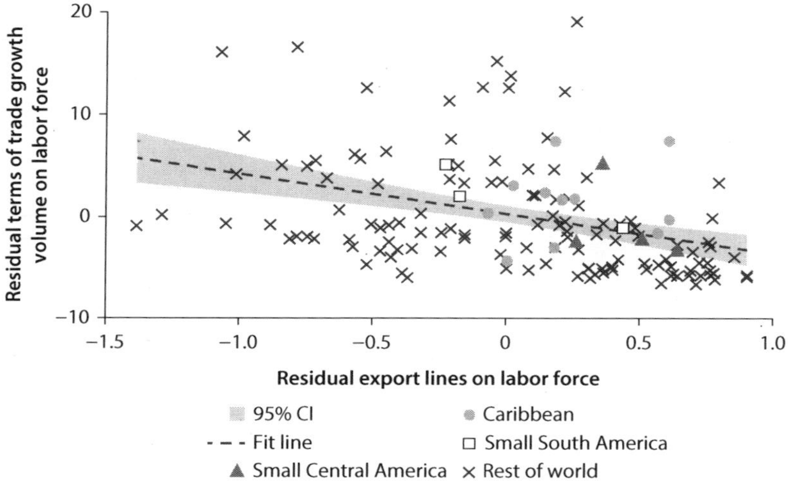

Sources: Calculations based on data from Penn World Table 8.1 (Feenstra, Inklaar, and Timmer 2015), World Bank World Development Indicators database, and UN COMTRADE data.
Note: The graph shows the fitted line of an ordinary least squares regression. It is estimated by first estimating the following two equations:
Log(std. dev. terms of trade growth) = log(labor force) + error1
Log(number of export lines) = log(labor force) + error2.
Then the plot represents the regression of error1 on error2. This can be thought of as representing the relation between the number of export lines and terms of trade volatility after removing the influence of labor force. The relationship is negative and significant at the 1 percent level with a coefficient of −4.091.

Figure 4.2 shows a statistically significant, negative relation between the number of products produced for export and terms of trade volatility, controlling for the impact of size. Figure 4.3 shows, perhaps unexpectedly, a statistically significant and positive relationship between size and terms of trade volatility, controlling for the average number of export product lines. These results, as well as results from the academic literature, seem to suggest that any impact small size has on terms of trade growth volatility occurs through the export concentration channel.

The linear regression results given in table 4.1 present more evidence suggesting that specialization plays a role in the high terms of trade volatility observed in small economies. Column 1 shows that the relationship between size and terms of trade growth rate volatility has a negative sign when not including any other controls. However, when controlling for the average annual number of export lines as well as average annual unique destination markets (two measures of specialization discussed in chapter 3), the coefficient on size turns positive, as shown in columns 2 and 3. These results are not definitive evidence that size does not directly increase terms of trade volatility in small economies, but they again suggest that the volatility stems from the export specialization channel. When controlling for either channel of specialization, size switches from a negative association with terms of trade growth rate volatility to a positive one. Columns 4, 5, and 6 show that the negative impact of having fewer export

Figure 4.3 Partial Correlation between Terms of Trade Volatility and Labor Force, Controlling for Number of Export Lines

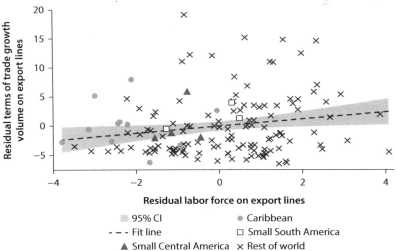

Source: Calculations based on data from Penn World Table 8.1 (Feenstra, Inklaar, and Timmer 2015), World Bank World Development Indicators database, and UN COMTRADE data.
Note: The graph shows the fitted line of an ordinary least squares regression. It is estimated by first estimating the following two equations:
Log(std. dev terms of trade growth) = log(average number of export lines) + error1
Log labor force = log(number of export lines) + error2.
Then the plot represents the regression of error1 on error2. This can be thought of as representing the relation between labor force size and terms of trade terms volatility after removing any impact from the number of export lines. The relationship is positive and significant at the 1 percent level with a coefficient of .639.

markets on terms of trade volatility is persistent when including export product concentration, development levels, and openness. The only term that retains significance throughout is the number of trading partners.

As noted above, the literature has focused for the most part on the role of concentration in export products as a source of terms of trade volatility. The relationship between export destinations and terms of trade volatility is less explored, but the regression results given in table 4.1 show that destinations may also play a role, as can be seen in column 7, where an interaction term is included. In this specification, the negative and statistically significant coefficient on the interaction term indicates that diversifications of partners and products are complements with respect to volatility. That is, the marginal effect of an additional product on terms of trade volatility varies systematically with the number of destinations. Alternatively, the marginal effect of the number of destinations depends on the number of products. This result is statistically significant at the 1 percent level; the number of products and the number of destinations are thus complements with respect to (reducing) terms of trade volatility. Further, the coefficients reported in column 6 can be interpreted as the average effects of each explanatory variable on terms of trade volatility. They show the marginal effect of each variable at the average of

Table 4.1 Determinants of Terms of Trade Volatility

Variables	(1) Terms of trade vol.	(2) Terms of trade vol.	(3) Terms of trade vol.	(4) Terms of trade vol.	(5) Terms of trade vol.	(6) Terms of trade vol.	(7) Terms of trade vol.
Working age population	−0.0988	0.582**	0.788***	0.788***	1.086***	0.859**	1.290***
	(0.206)	(0.246)	(0.259)	(0.262)	(0.341)	(0.354)	(0.399)
Number of export products		−4.026***		−0.00238	−0.839	−0.683	34.49***
		(0.835)		(2.040)	(2.204)	(2.171)	(8.417)
Number of destination markets			−7.391***	−7.387**	−8.352**	−8.434**	39.48***
			(1.393)	(3.476)	(3.453)	(3.453)	(12.06)
GDP per capita PPP					0.768	0.844	1.830***
					(0.600)	(0.611)	(0.686)
Openness						−1.213	−1.805*
						(0.965)	(0.955)
Interaction of export lines and markets							−8.215***
							(1.989)
Constant	8.613***	31.92***	41.20***	41.19***	43.16***	47.45***	−162.6***
	(0.547)	(4.997)	(6.317)	(6.704)	(6.998)	(8.196)	(51.42)
Observations	150	150	150	150	150	150	150
R-squared	0.001	0.141	0.172	0.172	0.185	0.191	0.295

Sources: Calculations based on data from Penn World Table 8.1 (Feenstra, Inklaar, and Timmer 2015), World Bank World Development Indicators database, Consolidated dataset on trade in services v8.8, and UN COMTRADE data.
Note: All variables in logs aside from terms of trade volatility. Robust standard errors in parentheses. *** $p<0.01$, ** $p<0.05$, * $p<0.1$.

the distribution, whereas the coefficients on log partners and log products in column 7 show the marginal impact of these variables when the other is 0.

Given that trade with 0 partners or in 0 products does not occur in the data, the practical relevance of the positive coefficients in column 7 is questionable. Figures 4.4 and 4.5 show the distributions of the marginal effects of the number of products and destinations across countries on terms of trade volatility. These figures show the predicted marginal effect of partners (products) conditional on the value of products (partners) for each country in the sample. Interestingly, figure 4.4 shows there are a few countries for which the marginal impact on terms of trade volatility of adding a partner is positive, given their low number of export products. That is, for these few economies, adding an additional partner results in more terms of trade volatility, given that they export few products (under the assumption that no new products would be added as a consequence of adding another export destination). Similarly, figure 4.5 shows there are some countries where the marginal impact of additional products on terms of trade volatility while holding the number of partners constant is positive. Note, however, that for most countries in our sample, the estimated marginal effect of additional partners (products) on terms of trade volatility is negative.

The results presented in this section are suggestive of the idea that the elevated terms of trade growth volatility seen in small economies comes through the channel of specialization rather than economic size directly. Thus diversification, in all of its forms, is a potential policy objective worth pursuing to counter terms of trade volatility. Furthermore, due in part to terms of trade volatility, small economies also face high levels of growth rate volatility, which is discussed next.

Figure 4.4 Marginal Impact of Partners, Given Number of Export Lines

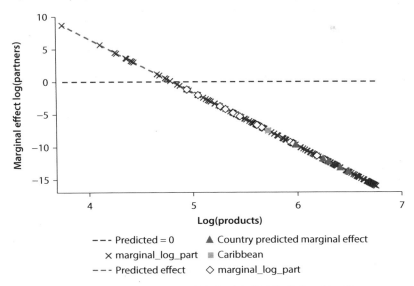

Sources: Calculations based on data from UN COMTRADE and the World Bank's Consolidated Data on International Trade in Services v8.8.
Note: The figure shows the marginal impact of a change in log(partners) conditional on log(export lines). The predicted line is calculated based on the coefficients reported in table 4.1, col. 7.

Figure 4.5 Marginal Impact of Products, Given Number of Trading Partners

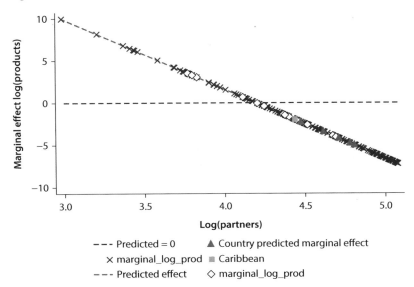

Sources: Calculations based on data from UN COMTRADE and the World Bank's Consolidated Data on International Trade in Services v8.8.
Note: The figure shows the marginal impact of a change in log(products) conditional on log(partners). The predicted line is calculated based on the coefficients reported in table 4.1, col. 7.

Volatility of Growth Rates

Growth rate volatility is a critical challenge to small economies, as it is correlated with negative long-run development and growth outcomes. However, as with terms of trade volatility, it does not appear to be related to size directly but to several characteristics of being a small economy, including the high levels of terms of trade volatility, which is due to export concentration, as discussed above, as well as openness.

The economics literature has recognized that a country's growth path may be important for development. Pritchett (2000) analyzes historical growth paths in developed and developing countries from 1960 to 1990, finding substantial variety in growth paths. He documents that while most developed countries experience slow and steady or steep continuous improvements in GDP per capita, which he calls "hills," developing countries are characterized by having much more unstable and volatile growth paths. Hausmann, Pritchett, and Rodrik (2004) analyze episodes of growth accelerations, which they define as eight-year periods in which growth increases at least 2 percent over the previous period and averages at least 3.5 percent a year. Strikingly, they find that more than half of countries in their global sample have experienced a growth acceleration. From these findings, it seems many countries can achieve positive growth rates for some period of time, but less-developed countries tend to struggle with volatility in their growth path. Indeed, Ramey and Ramey (1995) find that long-run growth is negatively correlated with growth rate volatility. Growth rate volatility thus seems to be a big part of the problem for countries exhibiting low levels of long-run growth rates.

Figure 4.6 shows growth rate volatility levels across size, income, and region country groupings. Looking at the distribution of median growth rate volatility over labor force size, GDP growth volatility seems to decline with labor force size in the upper half of the country-size distribution. This is borne out in figure 4.7, which shows the relationship between growth rate volatility and labor force size. The figure also shows a fit line estimated nonparametrically, which seems to indicate that there may be nonlinearity in the relationship. This may be due to the nonlinearity in the relationship between size and openness discussed in chapter 3. Figure 3.3 showed that really small countries seem to get more open as they get bigger, up to about 500,000 workers, before openness begins to decline with increasing size. The nonlinearity in figure 4.7 may be a related phenomenon, because, as discussed in the remainder of this subsection, growth volatility rises with openness.

The main feature of the distribution of growth rate volatility and income levels in figure 4.6 is what one would expect: OECD countries have experienced the least amount of long-run growth rate volatility. This is consistent with the literature discussed above on the differences in growth path among countries and the role of growth rate volatility in determining long-run development outcomes. Within LAC, countries in the Caribbean have experienced higher levels of growth volatility. This is unsurprising because, as is discussed below, terms of

Figure 4.6 Growth Rate Volatility, 1970–2013

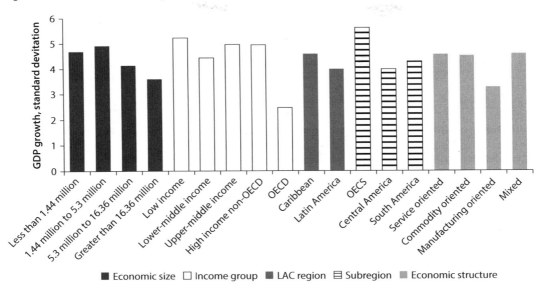

Source: Calculations based on data from the World Bank World Development Indicators database.
Note: Graph is constructed by first calculating annual growth in GDP per capita (2005 US$) for each year in the period 1970–2013 and then taking the standard deviation of the annual growth rate of GDP per capita (2005 US$) in each country over the period. The bar represents the median standard deviation of GDP per capita (2005 US$) annual growth rate among countries within each grouping.

Figure 4.7 Relationship between Size and Growth Volatility, 1970–2013

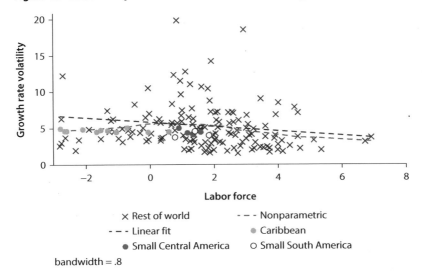

Source: Calculations based on data from the World Bank World Development Indicators database.
Note: The fitted line represents the predicted values of the following linear regression: std dev. GDP growth rate = log(labor force) + error. The coefficient on log(labor force) is −.303 and is significant at the 5 percent level. Outliers Bosnia and Herzegovina, Equatorial Guinea, Libya, and Oman were not included in the graph to improve visibility (but are included in regression lines).

trade volatility and openness to trade both appear to be determinants of growth rate volatility. The Caribbean has exhibited much higher terms of trade growth volatility and openness relative to Latin America. Manufacturing-oriented economies appear with discretely lower growth volatility than the other small LAC countries. This is likely due to the fact that the manufacturing-oriented group of countries only contains one Caribbean country, Haiti, which does not enter the sample until 1999.

The economics literature has identified several variables that may be relevant in understanding growth rate volatility, some of which were just discussed. Jansen (2004) finds that openness and terms of trade volatility, as well as export concentration through its effects on terms of trade volatility, are correlated with GDP growth volatility. A strong link has also been noted between terms of trade volatility and income volatility when controlling for the effects of high openness (Bacchetta et al. 2007). Acemoglu and Zilibotti (1997) find a fairly large negative relationship between development levels, as measured by GDP per capita, and GDP growth rate volatility. That is, more-developed countries tend to experience less growth rate volatility. In any discussion of the relationship between size and GDP growth rate volatility, the potential effect on growth rate volatility of all these variables must be accounted for, particularly terms of trade growth volatility and specialization. As discussed above, these variables are closely linked to size and represent an indirect channel through which size may impact growth rate volatility.

To begin the discussion of correlates with GDP growth rate volatility, consider table 4.2. The table, similar to table 4.1 in the previous section, shows regression results between many of the variables discussed in this book thus far and growth rate volatility. Column 1 shows the expected positive relationship between terms of trade volatility and growth rate volatility based on the literature just discussed. Column 2 shows that size is negatively correlated with growth rate volatility.

This negative relationship remains until the trade variables (export product/ market concentration and openness) are included in the regression, suggesting that size only has a negative impact on growth rate volatility through these variables. Columns 4 and 5 show that specialization in both export products and markets is negatively related to growth rate volatility. However, only the number of trading partners retains a weak significance once export product lines are included, and this disappears once openness is included in column 7. We also see that, unlike the case of terms of trade growth volatility, the interaction term between number of partners and products does not have a statistically significant relation with growth rate volatility.

While the results presented above are suggestive, they may suffer from issues of collinearity among the independent variables. Figure 4.8 shows graphically the partial correlation between terms of trade and growth rate volatility, controlling for development, size, openness, number of export lines, and number of export markets. The correlation is positive and significant, indicating that higher volatility in terms of trade growth is related to higher growth rate volatility.

Figure 4.9 shows the correlation between openness and growth rate volatility, controlling for size, development, terms of trade growth volatility, the number of

Table 4.2 Determinants of Growth Volatility

Variables	(1) Growth vol.	(2) Growth vol.	(3) Growth vol.	(4) Growth vol.	(5) Growth vol.	(6) Growth vol.	(7) Growth vol.
Standard deviation of terms of trade growth	0.175*** (0.0508)	0.170*** (0.0488)	0.157*** (0.0536)	0.0818** (0.0404)	0.0585 (0.0484)	0.0563 (0.0475)	0.0546 (0.0565)
Working age population		−0.433*** (0.151)	−0.448*** (0.149)	0.221 (0.266)	0.395 (0.297)	0.424 (0.303)	1.124*** (0.344)
GDP per capita PPP			−0.253 (0.258)	0.790 (0.621)	0.842 (0.596)	0.950 (0.646)	0.914* (0.533)
Number of export products				−3.674** (1.670)		−1.490 (1.769)	4.208 (7.786)
Number of destination markets					−6.625** (2.613)	−4.720* (2.546)	3.838 (8.668)
Openness							3.224*** (1.101)
Interaction of export lines and markets							−1.431 (1.580)
Constant	3.777*** (0.444)	4.586*** (0.531)	7.040*** (2.580)	19.28*** (5.212)	26.93*** (7.239)	26.18*** (6.779)	−22.09 (38.69)
Observations	150	150	150	150	150	150	150
R-squared	0.064	0.107	0.113	0.213	0.231	0.238	0.340

Sources: Calculations based on data from Penn World Table 8.1 (Feenstra, Inklaar, and Timmer 2015), World Bank World Development Indicators database, Consolidated dataset on trade in services v8.8, and UN COMTRADE data.
Note: All variables accept terms of trade growth volatility in logs. Robust standard errors in parentheses. *** $p<0.01$, ** $p<0.05$, * $p<0.1$.

export product lines, and the number of export markets. Again the results presented in table 4.2 hold, and openness appears to be positively related to growth rate volatility.

It is interesting to think through what channels terms of trade and openness might impact growth rate volatility. As noted in the previous section on terms of trade, many authors in the economics literature have noted the link between terms of trade volatility and growth outcomes. As one further example, Mendoza (1995) provides a formal analysis of the relationship between terms of trade volatility and growth rate volatility. He uses a business cycle model that includes terms of trade as well as productivity shocks and incorporates transmission mechanisms for terms of trade shocks via international capital mobility, the cost of imported inputs, and the overall purchasing power of exports. He finds that when including terms of trade shocks as well as productivity shocks, the model produces business cycles similar to those observed in the data. The relation between terms of trade volatility and growth volatility has been well studied both theoretically and empirically.

The channels through which openness can impact growth rate volatility are less clearly modeled. However, some basic insights can be gained by considering how openness is defined in this book, that is, total trade values as a percentage of GDP. The definition clarifies that openness is related to

Figure 4.8 Partial Correlation between Terms of Trade Volatility and Growth Rate Volatility, Controlling for Development, Size, Number of Export Lines, and Openness

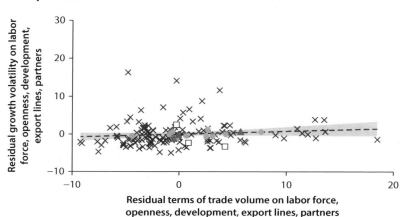

Sources: Calculations based on data from the World Bank World Development Indicators database, Penn World Table 8.1 (Feenstra, Inklaar, and Timmer 2015), and UN COMTRADE.
Note: The graph shows the fitted line of an ordinary least squares regression. It is calculated by first estimating the following two equations:
Std. dev. growth rate = log(openness) + log(labor force) + log(GDP per capita PPP) + log(number of export lines 1995–2013) + log(export markets 1995–2013) + error1;
Std. dev. terms of trade = log(openness) + log(labor force) + log(GDP per capita PPP) + log(number of export lines 1995–2013) + log(export markets 1995–2013) + error2.
Then the plot shows the regression of error1 on error2, which represents the relationship between terms of trade volatility and growth rate volatility after removing the impacts of openness, development, size, and the number of export lines produced. The relationship is positive with a coefficient of 0.077 that is significant at the 10 percent level.

growth rate volatility through changes in the total value of a country's trade flows. These flows, in turn, are related to the price a country receives for its goods and the quantity it sells, a function of demand for its products in export markets. This implies that the choices of export products and of destination markets are potentially important factors in determining how high levels of openness impact growth-rate volatility.

In fact, the impact of terms of trade volatility on growth volatility is related to the impact of openness on volatility. Changes in terms of trade represent changes in the relative price level of exports to imports in a given country, which in turn impact trade values. If trade values are a higher percentage of GDP (that is, the country is more open), then changes in trade values caused by movements in terms of trade should cause a larger movement in overall GDP. Thus, openness would seem to amplify the impact terms of trade volatility has on GDP volatility. In this context, diversification in export product lines could play an important role in reducing growth volatility. As discussed in the previous section, export diversification is associated with lower terms of trade volatility,

Figure 4.9 Partial Correlation between Openness and Growth Rate Volatility, Controlling for Development, Size, Number of Export Lines, and Terms of Trade Volatility

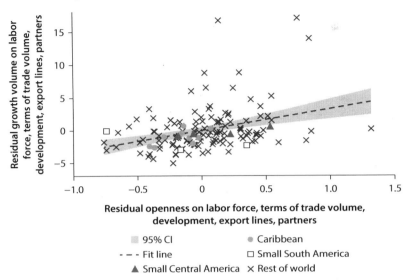

Sources: Calculations based on data from the World Bank World Development Indicators database, Penn World Table 8.1 (Feenstra, Inklaar, and Timmer 2015), and UN COMTRADE.
Note: The graph shows the fit line of an ordinary least squares regression. It is calculated by first estimating the following two equations:
Std. dev. growth rate = std. dev. terms of trade + log(labor force) + log(GDP per capita PPP) + log(average number of products exported) log(export markets 1995–2013) + error1
Log(openness)= std. dev. terms of trade + log(labor force) + log(GDP per capita PPP) + log(average number of export lines 1995–2013) + log(export markets 1995–2013) + error2.
Then the plot shows the regression of error1 on error2, which represents the relationship between openness and growth rate volatility after removing the impacts of terms of trade volatility, development, size, and the number of export lines produced. The relationship is positive with a coefficient of 3.354 that is significant at the 1 percent level.

which itself is associated with less growth rate volatility. These relationships between terms of trade volatility, export concentration, and growth rate volatility are well documented in the literature, as previously discussed.

A second channel through which openness potentially can impact growth volatility (a channel less documented in the economics literature) is by amplifying the impact of demand shocks or volatility in trading partner countries. The idea is that trade values are impacted by volatility or demand shocks in partner countries, and that openness will amplify any impact that this has on growth rate volatility. To the extent that countries become more vulnerable to shocks transferred from their partners as they become more dependent on particular export markets, diversification in terms of trading partners can play a role in reducing overall growth volatility.

There is some evidence in the literature consistent with the idea that trading partners might impact growth rate volatility. Frankel and Rose (1998) analyze data for 20 industrialized countries and find that the greater the trade linkages between countries, the more synchronized their business cycles are.

Calderon, Chong, and Stein (2007) expand the analysis to 147 developed and developing countries. They find a positive relationship between trade intensity and business cycle correlation for developing countries. They find a similar relationship in developed countries, although trade intensity seems to have a much smaller impact on business cycle correlation in that case. These findings are consistent with the idea that concentration of trade flows in a small number of partners may increase exposure to external sources of growth volatility. Kouame and Reyes (2015) analyze growth synchronization between countries in the Caribbean and major growth poles—China, Brazil, the European Union, and the United States. They find that countries in the Caribbean exhibit high degrees of synchronization with the growth cycles of the United States and the European Union and very little synchronization with the growth cycles of Brazil and China, which is reflective of the relative sizes of these countries as destination markets for Caribbean exports. Furthermore, in a theoretical context, Melitz (2003) emphasized that there may be high barriers to entry to new markets and that entry may occur over time. Under these conditions, it seems plausible that being highly concentrated in terms of export markets could result in a pass-through of volatility from importer to exporter, particularly if the costs of moving to other markets to make up for demand shortfalls is high.

In recently published work, Jansen, Lennon, and Piermartini (2016) make a first attempt at directly untangling the link between volatility at home and volatility in export markets by applying a Markowtiz-Tobin definition of portfolio risk to the selection of international trade partners. They create a measure of export partner risk that includes the variance and covariance of growth in all of a country's trading partners, weighted by the share each partner contributes to total exports. They find that their measure of export partner risk is highly correlated with growth volatility in the exporting country, even after controlling for several variables mentioned in this book, as well as time and country fixed effects.[1] This lends support to the idea that diversifying export markets may help reduce growth volatility. Interestingly, however, the authors also decompose their measure into the risks associated with the variance and covariance of growth in trading partners, finding covariance more important in determining growth rate volatility in the exporting country. Thus, while simple diversification of export markets may help, having stable export markets is necessary to minimize growth rate volatility. Nonetheless, the exact nature of the relationship between trading partners and growth volatility as well as possible channels through which it operates deserves further research.

The preceding sections showed that small economies face a significant challenge to economic growth in the form of high levels of economic volatility. However, this volatility does not seem to come directly as a result of small size, but rather through the high levels of openness and specialization associated with being small. While it is difficult to untangle the differing impact of specialization in export products and markets due to their high correlation, it seems that diversification in both of these areas could help reduce volatility.

There is, however, one more source of external volatility small economies face that defies an easy solution: Exposure to costly natural disasters, which is discussed next.

Higher Relative Costs of Natural Disasters

Although it may not seem to be the case when looking at the raw number of disaster occurrences, small economies face a disproportionate vulnerability to natural disasters when considering their costs relative to GDP. This is particularly true of small island states, where, when a disaster strikes, it often affects most of a country's centers of economic activity, leading to extremely high reconstruction costs.[2] These relatively high costs of natural disasters can contribute to the growth volatility discussed above, as well as to the fiscal challenges and low savings rates discussed in the sections following this one.

In understanding how natural disasters impact countries of different sizes, it is important to separate the concepts of exposure to disaster events and the relative costs of such events. Figure 4.10 documents the number of disasters per year of the median country in each grouping. Here, we see that it is larger economies and not smaller ones that seem to face more disaster events per year.[3] Thus it is not that smaller economies are more exposed to natural disasters per se. This makes sense, given the discussion in chapter 2 that land area is correlated roughly with labor force and population and, presumably, a larger land area makes a country more likely to experience an event

Figure 4.10 Number of Disasters per Year, 1970–2013

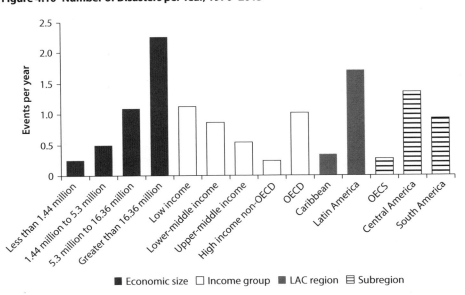

Sources: Calculations based on EM-DAT database and World Bank WDI.
Note: Bars represent the median value of the average number of disasters per year among countries within each grouping. We include years in which no disasters are reported in the EM-DAT data set as years in which no event occurred.

Open and Nimble • http://dx.doi.org/10.1596/978-1-4648-1042-8

somewhere in its territory. When looking at the distribution of disaster events across income levels, there does not appear to be a clear relationship between income and the number of disasters. While low-income countries generally experience more disasters, the OECD countries also have many events, indicating that it is possible to be rich and experience natural disasters. In LAC, we see that the Caribbean interestingly does not appear to experience many disasters relative to the rest of the region, and there are more disasters per year in the small economies of Central and South America than the OECS.

Turning to the issue of relative costs, figure 4.11 shows that despite having fewer events, it is smaller economies that bear the largest burden from disaster damages, measured relative to GDP. The figure shows, for years in which an event was recorded with a damage estimate in our data set, the average damage as a share of GDP in an event year for the median country in each grouping. We see in the distribution over labor force size groupings a reversal of the trend shown previously for the number of disasters: despite having fewer events, small economies experience higher relative costs from natural disasters when they occur. In fact, we may be underreporting this result, as our data set contains some events without a damage estimate and it seems that small economies are more likely to have these missing values.[4]

We see the same dynamic at play in Latin America and the Caribbean. Figure 4.10 above shows that Latin America experiences far more disaster

Figure 4.11   Damages Relative to GDP in a Disaster Year, 1970–2013

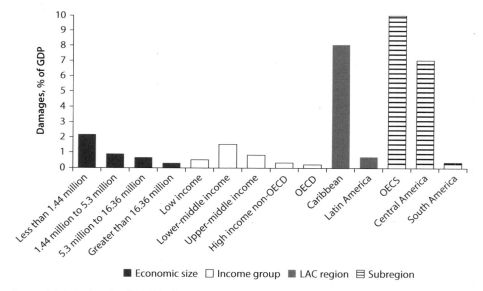

Sources: Calculations based on EM-DAT database and World Bank WDI.
Note: For ease of viewing other relationships, the y-axis of the figure has been cut off. The OECS actually has damages/GDP of around 19.6%. Bars are calculated by first calculating disaster damages/GDP for countries and years where a disaster and damage estimate are reported. These are averaged by country to represent the average cost of a disaster relative to GDP in the year it occurs. The bars then represent the median immediate cost of a disaster relative to GDP among countries within a group.

events than the Caribbean countries, whereas in figure 4.11 we see that relative costs are much higher in the Caribbean. We also see within the subregions of small LAC economies that Central America and the OECS experience the most damage relative to GDP.

The point that small economies face higher relative costs can also be seen in the regression results presented in table 4.3. Column 1 shows that having more events per year is associated with greater damages relative to GDP, and column 2 shows that when controlling for the number of events, working age population is negatively associated with damages. That is, small economies face higher relative costs of disasters. Further, the estimated coefficient on the frequency of disasters triples in size after controlling for the size of the working-age population, indicating that size matters in determining the relative damage from disasters.

In terms of the economics literature, there is some debate on the impact natural disasters have on a country's economic growth path in the long run, but there is a consensus that the short-run effects are negative.[5] Raddatz (2007) finds that climate events cause a drop in GDP of about 2 percent in the year a disaster occurs, and that all discernible impacts disappear some 3–5 years after the event. Strobl (2012) simulates disaster damage in the Caribbean at a local level using a wind weather forecasting model to account for potential measurement error in disaster damage reporting; the simulation shows highly localized short-run effects in the year after the disaster, which disappear shortly thereafter. The long-run impacts of disasters on growth are less clear. Skidmore and Toya (2002) find that disasters may have a positive impact on economic growth in the long run. The authors note that in their regressions, disasters are associated with increased productivity in an economy, and they theorize that there may be gains in upgrading destroyed physical capital in an economy. More recently, Hochrainer (2009) attempted to determine the impact of disasters on growth over a five-year time horizon by simulating counterfactual cases for various disasters. He finds that disasters have discernible negative effects on growth in the medium term.

The impact of disasters on economic growth seems to be highly dependent upon country characteristics. Noy (2009) finds that smaller economies

Table 4.3 Determinants of Damages from Disasters

Variables	(1) Average damages/GDP	(2) Average damages/GDP
Average events per year	0.476***	1.340***
	(0.136)	(0.201)
Working age population		−0.704***
		(0.121)
Constant	−6.414***	4.694**
	(0.163)	(1.923)
Observations	162	162
Adjusted R-squared	0.053	0.211

Sources: Calculations based on data from EM-DAT database and World Bank World Development Indicators database.
Note: All variables are in logs. Robust standard errors in parentheses. *** $p<0.01$, ** $p<0.05$, * $p<0.1$.

(in terms of GDP size) and developing countries face significantly higher output declines following a disaster of similar magnitude. The author finds that countries with higher literacy, higher per capita income, higher levels of openness, and higher levels of government spending are better able to withstand disasters. Additionally, countries with more foreign exchange reserves and higher levels of domestic credit seem to experience less of a growth effect from disasters. Noy theorizes this is because variables such as openness, development, and domestic credit generation imply an increased ability to mobilize resources for reconstruction efforts. Looking specifically at Caribbean economies, Rasmussen (2004) and Heger, Julca, and Paddiso (2008) find that short-run growth impacts are slightly larger than those found using global samples in the literature noted above.

Although much of the current research has focused on the relationship between natural disasters and GDP growth, several studies indicate that disasters can have much broader macroeconomic consequences in terms of fiscal balances, trade patterns, and consumption behavior. In his study of disaster impacts in the Caribbean, Rasmussen (2004) finds that natural disasters are associated with worsening external and fiscal balances and increased poverty. Ouattara and Strobl (2013) analyze the fiscal impact of hurricanes in the Caribbean and find that the typical hurricane strike significantly increases government spending and has a negative impact on the budget balance in the year it occurs. These findings are particularly relevant in the context of problems with high debt in small economies, which are discussed below. Gassebner, Keck, and Teh (2010) estimate a gravity model of global trade flows, including natural disasters as a control variable, and find that disasters significantly reduce both imports and exports. Auffret (2003) analyzes consumption volatility in the Caribbean. He finds that Caribbean economies experience significantly higher volatility of consumption than other countries in the world, likely due to the uncertainty caused by frequent natural disasters. He then analyzes 16 LAC countries and finds that disasters lead to substantial declines in investment growth and consumption growth. These are all potentially channels through which disasters could impact growth by affecting intermediate economic variables and deserve further study.

From the discussion above, it is clear that natural disasters represent an economically significant source of external growth volatility for small states, particularly small island states like those in the Caribbean, at least in the short run. Aside from direct impacts on GDP growth, they may also cause other macroeconomic problems. Disasters create trade and fiscal imbalances that can lead to higher levels of debt, and they may also decrease savings and investment in the region due to the uncertainty they cause. Thus, the higher relative costs of natural disasters small economies face are important not just as a source of external volatility. They may also contribute to the remaining two challenges small economies face: challenges of fiscal management and low long-term savings rates.

Fiscal Challenges in the Context of Fixed Exchange Rates

In addition to the challenges posed by volatility, small economies face challenges in managing public finances. Small countries typically face a high cost of providing public services due to the inability to exploit economies of scale in the production of public goods, as discussed in chapter 3. In addition, LAC economies in particular show low levels of revenue generation relative to the rest of the world. These two factors create an environment favorable to the accumulations of high levels of public debt, particularly in LAC small economies. Combined with the external volatility discussed above, these issues of public finances can contribute to lower long-run savings and ultimately lower long-run growth potential in small economies.

The Choice of Exchange Rate Regime

Economists typically tout the benefits of a flexible or floating exchange rate regime for facilitating adjustments in an economy. However, many people living in small economies feel differently. The argument is that one way in which small states might seek to manage their exposure to the economic volatility discussed above is through the choice of a fixed exchange rate regime, which can provide a stable anchor for prices in the economy.

In fact, as the title of this section indicates, many small economies do opt to fix their exchange rate in some way or another. Figure 4.12 represents the share of country-year observations that exhibit a particular exchange rate regime over the period 1996–2007 for different country size groupings, where the exchange rate becomes more flexible as the x axis increases. It is evident from these distributions of exchange rate regime by country size that smaller economies tend to exhibit relatively more cases of fixed or tightly managed exchange rate regimes than larger ones. However, the question still remains: Are these small economies making the best choice of exchange rate regime in terms of both managing volatility and having effective fiscal policy?

There are several plausible reasons to believe that small states benefit less from floating exchange rates and that a fixed exchange rate may even be optimal. As discussed earlier in this book, small states appear to suffer from a lack of economies of scale in the public sector. This implies that managing a central bank, providing workers with the necessary technical expertise to run monetary policy, and having the financial architecture in place to conduct monetary policy interventions may be difficult. Imam (2010) studies the issue of exchange rate choice in a sample of 61 "microstates" (defined as countries with a population of less than 2 million) and finds results consistent with the idea that scale matters in deciding which exchange rate regime to institute. Specifically, he conducts probit regression analysis and finds that within this sample, the smaller states are more likely to undergo full dollarization. Imam interprets dollarization as a move that allows countries to avoid the costs of establishing their own monetary policy and staffing a central bank with experts.

Open and Nimble • http://dx.doi.org/10.1596/978-1-4648-1042-8

Figure 4.12 Choice of Exchange Rate Regime by Labor Force, 1996–2007

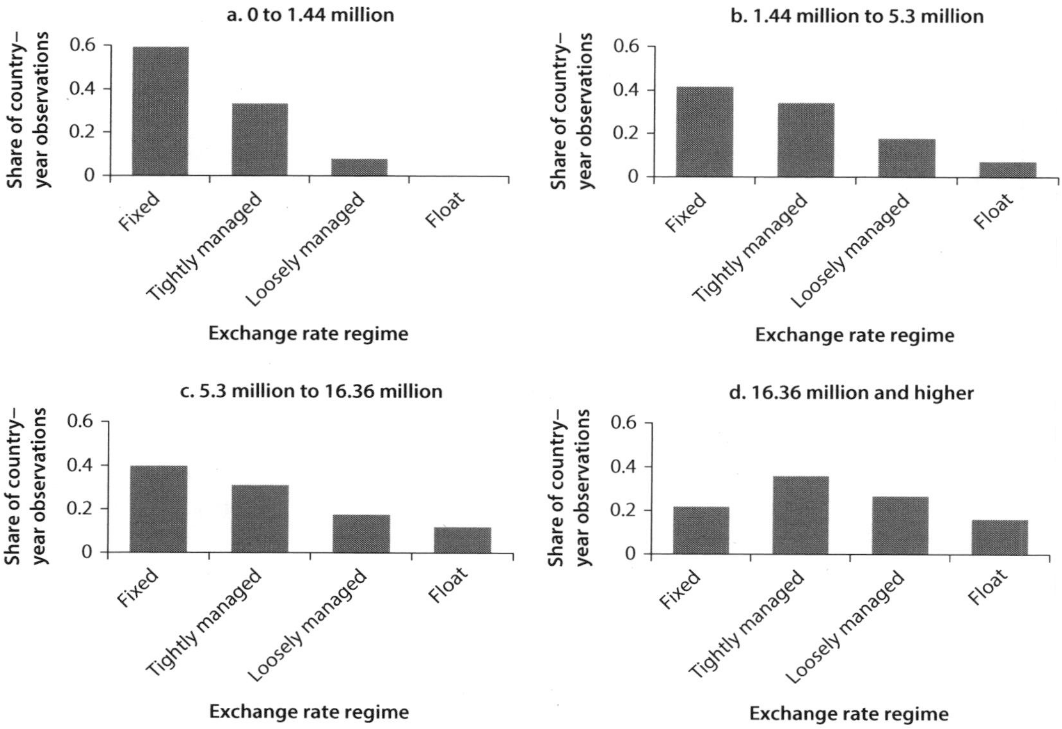

Sources: Calculations based on exchange rate regime data from Rienhart and Rogoff (2004) and World Bank World Development Indicators.
Note: The figure shows the share of country-year observations of a given exchange rate regime by country size groupings over the period 1995–2007. Exchange rate regime classifications are based on Rienhart and Rogoff (2004).
Fixed *includes* no separate tender, pre-announced peg or currency board, pre-announced horizontal band narrower or equal ±2 percent, de facto peg
Tightly managed *includes* pre-announced crawling peg, pre-announced crawling band narrower or equal ±2 percent, de facto crawling peg, de facto crawling band narrower or equal ±2 percent
Loosely managed *includes* pre-announced crawling band wider or equal ±2 percent, de facto crawling band narrower or equal ±5 percent, moving band that is narrower or equal to ±2 percent, managed floating
Float *includes* floating and cases of hyperinflation.

The role of the exchange rate in facilitating real adjustments may also have to be reconsidered in small economies. As noted in chapter 3, such economies tend to be highly specialized in production. As a result, they import a relatively large amount of primary goods, such as food and fuel. This holds particularly for small island states, which may lack the land needed to produce food. As demand for these goods is often inelastic, and the domestic production of these goods is quite small, it is not clear that exchange rate movements would facilitate adjustment in their usual way. Imam (2008) analyzes the process of current account adjustments in micro states (defined as just noted above). He finds, surprisingly, that the impact of a depreciation of the real effective exchange rate on the current account is not statistically significant for micro states (but is negative and significant for a global sample of countries). The results imply that a main channel through which flexible exchange rates help reduce economic volatility is not active in states with less than 2 million people. This finding is consistent with the idea just discussed that small states may violate the Marshall-Lerner condition. That is, their imports and exports are not elastic enough with respect to the exchange rate for exchange rate movements to induce reallocation and adjustment of economic activity.

A third point is that the outsized role of trade and investment flows in small economies may make having a flexible or floating exchange rate regime more difficult. Given the outsized role of trade and FDI relative to GDP (see the discussion on openness in chapter 5), even a nominally floating exchange rate would likely have to be heavily managed to ensure economic stability, resulting in limited monetary flexibility in practice. Related to this point, as these economies have relatively small domestic markets and therefore small amounts of domestic currency in circulation at any given time, their foreign exchange markets are likely to be sensitive to relatively small inflows of foreign currency. Given the outsized role of FDI and trade just noted, this could lead to significant volatility and provide another source of uncertainty in the economy.

Klein and Shambaugh (2006) document the fact that exchange rate regimes do matter for volatility and that fixed exchange rate regimes tend to exhibit less volatility than more flexible regimes. Breedon, Petursson, and Rose (2011) analyze the choice of exchange rate regime in the case of small, rich economies. They find that most of these countries have adopted some form of fixed rate regime and those that have not seem to experience more exchange rate volatility without any changes in underlying economic volatility.[6] In the context of small states that are highly open to trade and FDI inflows, avoiding this exchange rate volatility may be beneficial in terms of reducing overall economic volatility.

However, these potential benefits in reducing volatility do not come without costs. Having a fixed exchange rate policy implies that all economic adjustments have to be carried out through fiscal policy, which limits policy makers' options when responding to economic crises. Furthermore, Ilzetzki, Mendoza, and Vegh (2013) provide evidence that the exchange regime and country characteristics can influence the impact fiscal policy itself has on the economy. These authors find that while countries operating under fixed exchange rate regimes generally have higher fiscal multipliers, countries which are highly open tend to have smaller multipliers. Furthermore, those that have high levels of debt may even exhibit negative fiscal multipliers, meaning that public spending to boost the economy may actually have a net negative effect on growth. Given that small economies are highly open (discussed further in chapter 5), and that some small economies have high debt levels (discussed in the next section), it is unclear whether or not a fixed exchange rate regime will be a net positive in practice for these economies. It may even be a net negative, to the extent that the high openness and debt levels in small economies have a negative impact on the effectiveness of fiscal policy.

In sum, there are plausible arguments supporting the idea that moving toward a tightly managed or fixed exchange rate can be beneficial for small economies. In particular, for countries with less than 2 million people, concerns about economies of scale in central banking and the size of the nontradable sector may indicate that a tightly managed or fixed exchange is more prudent to manage economic volatility and prices. However, this choice may severely limit policy makers' ability to influence the economy, particularly in the context of high debt discussed below.

High Levels of Public Debt

Given the higher relative cost of government in small economies, as well as their higher relative costs of natural disasters and exposure to external volatility discussed previously, it is perhaps not surprising that many small economies seem to face high debt burdens.

Figure 4.13 shows the median level of gross government debt in 2013 by different country groupings. Based on the distribution of debt levels by labor force size, there is not a clear relationship between size and debt levels, though it seems the smallest countries have significantly more debt relative to GDP than the rest. Looking at the distribution of debt over income groupings, debt levels seem to rise with income. This is likely due to the fact (discussed in chapter 3) that higher-income countries exhibit better revenue generation and therefore may be perceived as less risky borrowers. It also may be related to lower external volatility in high-income countries, particularly the OECD, as was discussed earlier in this chapter. Within LAC, the Caribbean has a very large problem with debt levels relative to other small states in the region, the reason for which is discussed later in this section. Other small LAC countries tend to follow the pattern established by size. Finally, service-oriented small economies in LAC have high levels

Figure 4.13 Government Debt in 2013

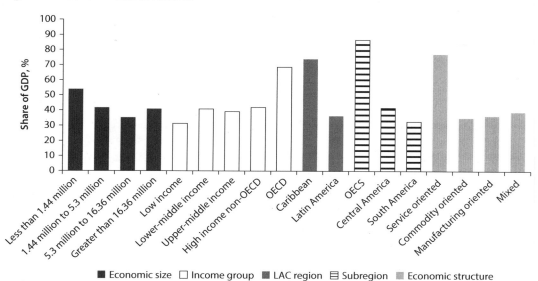

Source: Calculations based on April 2015 data from the IMF World Economic Outlook database.
Note: Bars represent the median value of the ratio of gross government debt to GDP in 2013 among countries in each grouping.

of debt, but this is because the majority of the countries making up these groupings are in the Caribbean.

The economics literature tells us that high levels of debt are potentially important for growth. Caner, Grennes, and Koehler-Geib (2010) investigate the idea of a "tipping point" debt-to-GDP ratio, after which growth rates become negatively impacted by high debt burdens. In a sample of 101 developed and developing countries, they find that long-run growth begins to exhibit a negative relationship with debt if long-run debt is greater than 77 percent of GDP. They also note that the threshold is significantly lower for developing countries, a debt level of around 64 percent of GDP, and that it potentially varies by country based on factors such as the development of domestic financial markets.

Although there seems to be some consensus that debt is important for growth, determining precise mechanisms and causality is difficult. Many in the literature point to the idea of the existence of a debt overhang. Theoretically, Krugman (1988) defines the issue as "the presence of inherited debt sufficiently large that creditors do not expect with confidence to be fully repaid." He notes that this situation distorts incentives and may lead to several scenarios that hinder growth, including a lack of commitment by the debtor government to enact domestic policy reforms if the gains are perceived to go mainly to foreign creditors, and a tendency for creditors to continue lending in order to ensure repayments of their previous debts. Deshpande (1995) investigates one practical implication of this theory, the idea that high levels of debt reduce investment, and finds evidence that this is the case in a sample of 13 severely indebted countries. Pattillio, Poirson, and Ricci (2004) investigate the issue of debt overhang further, finding that in fact high levels of debt are associated with lower productivity and reduced capital investment. Furthermore, their results indicate a causal relationship in which high debt causes lower growth and not the other way around. In trying to determine a causal relationship between growth and debt, Panizza and Presbitero (2014) use the fact that exchange rate movements change the value of foreign currency–denominated debt to construct an instrumented variable for public debt. They find no evidence that higher government debt causes lower growth. They do, however, find a significant relationship between the two. Although the direction of causality is unclear, there is some consensus that low growth and high debt tend to happen together.

As hinted at above, although debt levels do not seem to be related to size directly, they are related to terms of trade volatility. Figure 4.14 shows this correlation, which is negative and statistically significant at the 1 percent level.

Figure 4.15 shows that this negative relationship retains its significance when accounting for the effects of size and levels of development. This negative relation may be because there is a perception that economies with high terms of trade volatility carry greater risk and therefore have a harder time getting debt financing. In fact, recent work has shown that higher terms of trade volatility is associated with reduced ability to tap into international capital markets

Figure 4.14 Relationship between Government Debt and Terms of Trade Volatility

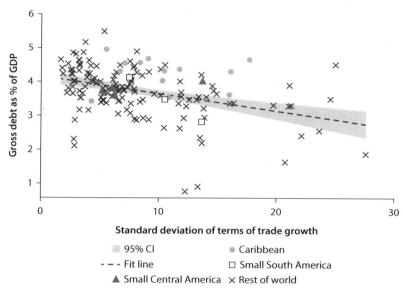

Sources: Calculations based on data from the Penn World Table 8.1 (Feenstra, Inklaar, and Timmer 2015) and April 2015 data from the IMF World Economic Outlook database.
Note: The figure shows the fit line of the following linear regression:
Log(gross government debt/GDP) = std. dev terms of trade growth + error
The relationship is negative and statistically significant at the 1 percent level with a coefficient of –0.0513.

(Gelos, Sahay, and Sandleris 2011). There is also a statistically significant correlation between debt levels and GDP growth rate volatility, which again could indicate that volatility impacts a country's perceived ability to pay back debt.[7] Interestingly, most of the Caribbean economies are significantly above the trend line and outside of the confidence interval in figure 4.15. That is, they have much more debt than predicted based on their terms of trade volatility alone. The fact that countries in the region receive significantly more debt than predicted by their volatility levels raises questions about who is lending them money and why countries in the region can hold such large amounts of debt relative to GDP.

In the context of this book, several plausible explanations for high debt levels in the Caribbean emerge. The first is the region's exposure to external economic volatility, which would tend to lead to countercyclical government spending policies in order to smooth consumption patterns; this view is argued by Rodrik (1998). Within the discussion of external volatility above, it would also seem that natural disasters are particularly relevant for the Caribbean, given their relatively large levels of disaster damage as a share of GDP. These events can cause massive destruction of economic capital and require large outlays for rebuilding capital and infrastructure, as well as humanitarian assistance programs. Typically, disasters result in emergency loans being made by lenders that might not be as concerned about a country's ability to pay back the loan.

Figure 4.15 Partial Correlation between Government Debt and Terms of Trade Volatility, Controlling for GDP per Capita Levels, Labor Force Size, and Openness

Sources: Calculations based on data from the Penn World Table 8.1 (Feenstra, Inklaar, and Timmer 2015), World Bank World Development Indicators, and April 2015 data from the IMF World Economic Outlook database.

Note: The figure shows the fit line of an ordinary least squares regression. It is calculated by first estimating the following two equations:

Log(gross government debt/GDP) = log(GDP per capita PPP) + log(labor force) + error1

Std. dev. terms of trade growth = log(GDP per capita PPP) + log(labor force) + error2

Then the plot represents the regression of error1 on error2. This can be thought of as representing the relation between terms of trade volatility and the ratio of government debt to GDP when removing the effects of both labor force size and GDP per capita PPP. The relationship is negative with a coefficient of −0.0582 and is significant at the 1 percent level.

Finally, as these levels of debt have built up over time, it may be the case that countries in the region experience negative debt dynamics. Debt levels initially elevated by natural disasters or due to some other reason may take on a life of their own through ever-increasing interest rate payments.

In fact, in a recent report on public sector debt in the Caribbean, the Caribbean Development Bank (2014) conducts an accounting exercise of debt growth in the region since the 1990s and finds support for negative debt dynamics and natural disasters as drivers of debt.[8] They note that changes in public debt level from year to year can be broken down into the sum of the government's primary balance in a given year, interest payments made on previous debt, exchange rate movements changing the value of outstanding foreign debt, and other events. "Other events" in this case are said to capture the impact on the central government of contingent liabilities such as public company debt, bailouts, and other instances where the central government assumes debt it did not contract, a common occurrence in the Caribbean. The report further separates the government's primary balance into two components, in an attempt to capture the role of natural disasters and foreign aid in increasing the region's public debt. There is a basic balance component, made up of regularly occurring revenue minus expenses, and a capital balance component, made up of grant revenue minus all nonrecurrent transaction and capital expenditures.

For the seven countries that have accumulated more debt than GDP over the last two decades, the Caribbean Development Bank finds heterogeneity in what caused increasing debt levels between countries. However, on average, interest rate payments on previous debt and other events accounted for the clear majority of debt increases during this period. In fact, on average, these countries had large basic balance surpluses, but these were counterbalanced by large capital balance deficits, precipitated by frequent natural disasters. Thus, the overall government primary balance remained fairly neutral with regard to debt level changes. Real exchange rate movements were largely favorable and would have reduced debt value on their own during this period. The implications of these findings for policy in the Caribbean are discussed in chapter 6.

In summary, small economies have large fiscal challenges. They often exhibit high debt levels related to, at least in part, their inability to obtain economies of scale in the provision of public goods; their exposure to external volatility; and the high relative costs of natural disasters, which necessitate unexpected spending. This challenge of high debt levels is particularly difficult for small economies in LAC, which face the additional constraint of low government revenue generation. These high levels of public debt can limit long-term growth potential in small economies by lowering investment and contributing to low long-run savings rates, a topic discussed in the following section.

Low Savings Rates

Given these challenges to public sector financial management, it is perhaps not surprising that small economies tend to exhibit low savings rates. Small LAC economies in particular struggle with low domestic savings. The challenges of external volatility and fiscal management discussed above have contributed to a long-term pattern of low domestic savings rates in small economies. In addition to further limiting the flexibility small economies have when dealing with their external volatility and natural disaster exposure, low levels of savings may impact long-run growth potential through a reduction in investment levels. Together, these issues constitute an important challenge to establishing stable, long-term GDP growth.

Figure 4.16 shows the distribution of the median average annual savings rate from 1970 to 2013 for different country groupings. From the distribution of savings rates over labor force size groupings, it appears that larger countries save a lot more than the rest as a percentage of GDP. This is reinforced by figure 4.17, which shows a regression of size against long-run savings rate; the results suggest that there is a positive association between these variables, and bigger countries tend to save more.[9] From the distribution of savings over income groups, it seems that higher-income countries save more.

Open and Nimble • http://dx.doi.org/10.1596/978-1-4648-1042-8

Figure 4.16 Long-Run Savings, 1970–2013

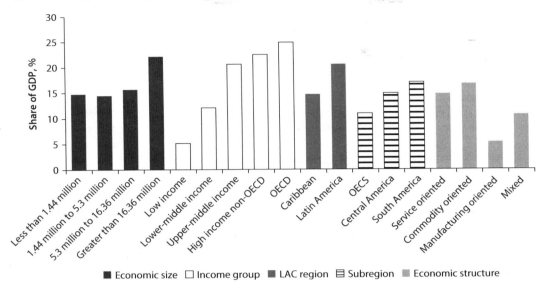

Source: Calculations based on data from World Development Indicators database.
Note: Bars in the figure represent the median value of average savings/GDP ratio from 1970 to 2013 among countries within each grouping.

Figure 4.17 Savings Rate versus Size

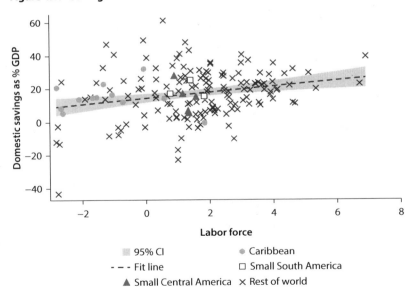

Source: Calculations based on data from World Development Indicators database.
Note: The figure shows the fit line of the following linear regression:
Gross domestic savings rate/GDP = log(labor force) + error
The relationship is positive and statistically significant at the 1 percent level with a coefficient of 1.821 on labor force size. Outliers dropped from the sample: Liberia, Lesotho, and Timor-Leste. Results available upon request.

In terms of LAC, economies in the Caribbean exhibit markedly lower savings rates than the rest of Latin America. Other small LAC economies seem to follow the pattern dictated by their size.

From the discussion preceding this section, there are several reasons why savings would tend to be lower in small economies. On the public side, part of the explanation for the low savings rate in small economies lies with the impact of size directly on government spending. Small size limits access to economies of scale in the provision of public goods leading to higher relative costs for providing public services. Economies in LAC face the additional challenge of low revenue generation in the region, as discussed in chapter 3.

The high exposure to natural disasters, particularly in small island economies like the Caribbean, also may play a role by forcing governments into unplanned expenditures which reduce public savings capacity. All of these factors are plausible contributors to low levels of public savings.

On the private side, low savings in small economies can be explained using theories from behavioral economics. Kahneman and Tversky (1979) note that people tend to evaluate decisions in terms of changes from the status quo rather than looking at longer-term gains and losses. In the context of small economies, people may be called upon to frequently re-evaluate savings and consumption behavior due to high growth rate volatility and terms of trade volatility. Enhancing this tendency is the aforementioned high relative costs of natural disasters. When a person is called upon to frequently re-evaluate their decisions, myopic (short-sighted) behavior tends to increase. Given that people tend to overweight the present and exhibit loss aversion when making decisions, they may exhibit lower-than-optimal savings. Each time they re-evaluate their savings/consumption decision, they are no longer thinking about a longer-term time horizon but are evaluating losses and gains from current levels of consumption.[10]

Looking at the median average annual savings rate distribution across income groups in figure 4.16, it seems that higher-income countries save significantly more than lower-income countries. Figures 4.18 and 4.19 together show one potential reason for this trend. Figure 4.18 shows statistically significant positive associations between domestic savings and investment, and figure 4.19 shows associations between investment and growth on the right. The idea is that higher domestic savings rates lead to more investment by making more capital available for investment projects. These investments in productive capacity in turn lead to higher long-term growth rates, which in turn provide greater scope for increased savings levels.

The correlations are consistent with research by de la Torre and Ize (2015), showing that domestic savings plays an important role in determining investment conditions and growth rates in the medium term, partly by reducing the cost of capital. Another potential channel through which savings impacts growth is innovation. Aghion et al. (2016) propose a theoretical model in which growth in a country requires innovation, which itself requires the pairing of a local investor with a foreign investor who brings knowledge of state-of-the-art technology. In this scenario, domestic savings matters a lot for growth in poorer countries and

Figure 4.18 Relationship between Savings and Investment

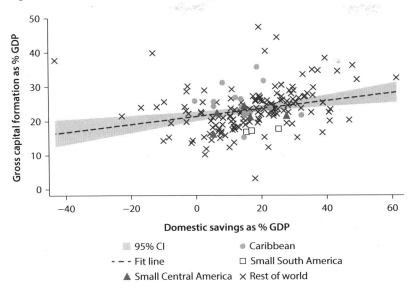

Source: Calculations based on data from World Bank World Development Indicators database.
Note: The figure shows the fit line of the following linear regression:
Gross capital formation/GDP = domestic savings/GDP + error
The relationship is positive and statistically significant at the 5 percent level with a coefficient of .115
Outliers dropped from the sample: Equatorial Guinea, Liberia, Lesotho, Micronesia, Timor-Leste. Results available upon request.

Figure 4.19 Relationship between Investment and Growth

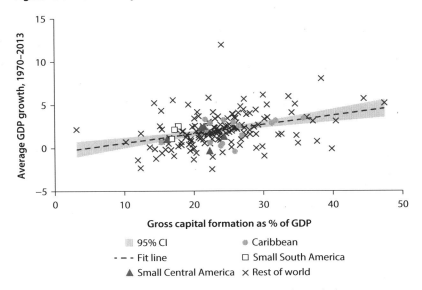

Source: Calculations based on data from World Bank World Development Indicators database.
Note: The figure shows the fit line of the following linear regression:
GDP growth per capita (2005 US$) = gross capital formation/GDP + error
The relationship is positive and statistically significant at the 1 percent level with a coefficient of .106.
Outlier dropped from the sample: Equatorial Guinea. Results available upon request.

less so in richer countries. Indeed these authors find evidence that domestic savings is strongly correlated with growth in poorer countries, and less so in richer ones which they interpret as supportive of their model.

If these authors are correct and domestic savings matters for growth, than the Caribbean countries, given their low savings rates shown in figure 4.16 relative to Latin America and other country groupings, should experience low growth. Looking again at figure 2.4, there is some evidence of slow long-term growth rates in the Caribbean consistent with this theory, particularly if one looks at growth rates in the period since 1990, as noted in the introduction. If low levels of investment are the cause of slow growth in the region, one way to increase growth should be to supplement domestic investment with foreign inflows, something that small economies generally and Caribbean economies in particular are already doing, as is discussed in the next chapter.

Notes

1. Controls used by Jansen, Lennon, and Piermartini (2016) include an HHI for product concentration, GDP per capita, population, openness, government expenditure, financial openness, real exchange rate volatility, terms of trade volatility, civil war, and military intervention. The authors also include country and year fixed effects and an interaction of openness and their measure of export partner risk.

2. One reason why relative measures of exposure are important emerges from the U.S. experience. The United States recorded the largest raw number of disasters and has experienced the largest total damages over the period 1970–2013. Yet it is not a country typically thought of as being strongly impacted by natural disasters. This is because the costs of these events in such a large country are spread among more people and over a much larger area. This leads to a lower likelihood that a disaster will strike key economic centers and an ability to engage in internal risk sharing, whereby one part of the country unaffected by the disaster can subsidize the recovery effort of the disaster-struck area. Risk-sharing options for small economies in LAC are discussed in chapter 6.

3. In constructing figure 4.10, there is a potential issue with the EM-DAT database, because it does not report any years in which zero disasters occur. To correct for this, we assume that any years which do not report an event in the EM-DAT data set are years when no event occurred and include them as years reporting 0 events. While we feel this is a valid assumption, we acknowledge that it may bias the results if, for example, large countries are systematically more likely to report events that occur relative to smaller ones.

4. The EM-DAT database contains a large number of disaster occurrences for which no damage figure is reported. Damages reported are estimates in the year of the event, and to the extent that small economies are unable to quickly estimate disaster damages relative to large economies, the results in figure 4.11 may be underrepresenting their true disaster-related costs. Running a simple probit model shows that, conditional on an event being reported, a countries (log) working age population is positively related to the observation of a damage estimate, with a coefficient of .185 that is statistically significant at the 1 percent level. This suggests that it is indeed the case that we are underreporting damages in small economies in the text.

5. For a comprehensive review of the economic impact of natural disasters, see Cavallo and Noy (2011).

6. These authors define small, rich economies as those with a population between 30,000 and 3 million and a GDP per capita PPP (in 2007) of at least $11,500.

7. The regression of std. dev. GDP growth on log(gross debt/GDP) yields a coefficient of −.068 that is significant at the 1 percent level.

8. Countries included in the exercise are Antigua and Barbuda, Barbados, Belize, Dominica, Grenada, Jamaica, and St. Kitts and Nevis. "Other events" was the largest contributor to debt increases on average, and the only factor that was significant in all seven countries. With regard to heterogeneity of the debt paths, it was found that Belize, Grenada, and St. Kitts and Nevis saw their debt increase in large part due to deteriorating fiscal balances, partly related to hurricane strikes and the subsequent increase in capital expenditure. Antigua and Barbuda and Jamaica were the only two countries in the sample in which interest payments on previously incurred debt played a significant role in increasing their debt levels over time, despite governments there achieving primary budget surpluses. Dominica's rising debt levels seem to reflect equal contributions from all the above-mentioned factors. Barbados is the only country in the group for which "other events" is the only significant source of increasing debt levels.

9. There were some outliers in the savings and investment data not included in regressions in this section. Outliers in the savings data include Lesotho, Liberia, and Timor-Leste. Outliers in the investment data include Equatorial Guinea. These were determined to be outliers visually on a two-way scatter plot and by the fact that they lay more than three times the interquartile range below the 25th percentile or above the 75th percentile in the data series.

10. Behavioral economists note that people regularly exhibit myopia (bias toward the present moment) and loss aversion when making decisions. Loss aversion, the idea that people value losses more than gains, was first proposed as part of prospect theory by Kahneman and Tversky (1979). In contrast to traditional economic theory, utility is thought of as being related to changes in wealth or consumption from a baseline (such as the current level) rather than as increasing levels generally. The relevance of this distinction is discussed by Benartzi and Thaler (1995) and applied to the equity premium puzzle. The puzzle is that stocks command a significantly greater return than bonds over long time horizons, and yet investors still choose to invest in bonds long term. The authors resolve this through the idea of loss aversion and myopia. They theorize that the frequency with which investors are forced to check their portfolio (typically when annual reports are sent out by financial intuitions) becomes the time horizon they use to make decisions on their investments, regardless of the time horizon they set out to invest for (for example, retirement in 30 years). Whenever people evaluate their portfolio, they exhibit loss aversion and avoid potential losses more than they value gains. When evaluating changes over a yearly period, bonds are much more attractive then stocks because they are relatively risk free over a given year (as opposed to stocks, which can swing wildly yearly but in the long run average a higher return). Thus, people investing for retirement in 30 years still own a large percentage of low-return bonds. In a follow-up experimental paper, Thaler et al. (1997) presented participants with a decision to invest in a low-risk or high-risk fund and paid them at the end of the experiment based on their performance. They found that participants who got the most frequent feedback during the process took the least risk and earned the least money.

References

Acemoglu, Daron, and Fabrizio Zilibotti. 1997. "Was Prometheus Unbound by Chance? Risk, Diversification, and Growth." *Journal of Political Economy* 105 (4): 709–51.

Aghion, Philippe, Diego Comin, Peter Howitt, and Isabel Tecu. 2016. "When Does Domestic Savings Matter for Economic Growth?" *IMF Economic Review* 64 (3): 381–407.

Auffret, Philippe. 2003. "High Consumption Volatility: The Impact of Natural Disasters?" Working Paper 2962, World Bank, Washington, DC.

Bacchetta, Marc, Marion Jansen, Roberta Piermartini, and Alberto Amurgo-Pacheco. 2007. "Export Diversification as an Absorber of External Shocks." Unpublished paper, World Trade Organization, Geneva.

Breedon, Francis, Thorarinn Petursson, and Andrew K. Rose. 2011. "Exchange Rate Policy in Small Rich Economies." Central Bank of Iceland Working Paper 53, Reykjavic.

Calderon, Cesar, Alberto Chong, and Ernesto Stein. 2007. "Trade Intensity and Business Cycle Synchronization: Are Developing Countries any Different?" *Journal of International Economics* 71: 2–21.

Caner, Mehmet, Thomas Grennes, and Fritzi Koehler-Geib. 2010. "Finding the Tipping Point: When Sovereign Debt Turns Bad." Policy Research Working Paper 5391, World Bank, Washington, DC.

Caribbean Development Bank. 2014. "Public Sector Debt in the Caribbean: An Agenda for Reduction and Sustainability." Caribbean Development Bank, St. Michael, Barbados.

Cavallo, Eduardo, and Ilan Noy. 2011. "Natural Disasters and the Economy—A Survey." *International Review of Environmental and Resource Economics* 5: 63–102.

De la Torre, Augusto, and Alain Ize. 2015. "Should Latin America Save More to Grow Faster?" Policy Research Working Paper 7386, World Bank, Washington, DC.

Deshpande, Ashwini. 1995. "The Debt Overhang and the Disincentive to Invest." *Journal of Development Economics* 52 (1): 169–87.

Feenstra, Robert C., Robert Inklaar, and Marcel P. Timmer. 2015. "The Next Generation of the Penn World Table." *American Economic Review* 105 (10): 3150–82. http://www.ggdc.net/pwt.

Frankel, Jeffrey, and Andrew Rose. 1998. "The Endogeneity of the Optimum Currency Area Criteria." *Economic Journal* 108 (449):1009–25.

Gassebner, Martin, Alexander Keck, and Robert Teh. 2010. "Shaken, Not Stirred: The Impact of Disasters on International Trade." *Review of International Economics* 18 (2): 351–68.

Gelos, R. Gaston, Ratnas Sahay, and Guido Sandleris. 2011. "Sovereign Borrowing by Developing Countries: What Determines Market Access?" *Journal of International Economics* 83: 243–54.

Hausmann, Ricardo, Lant Pritchett, and Dani Rodrik. 2004. "Growth Accelerations." NBER Working Paper 10566, National Bureau of Economic Research, Cambridge, MA.

Heger, Martin, Alex Julca, and Oliver Paddison. 2008. "Analyzing the Impact of Natural Hazards in Small Economies: The Caribbean Case." Working Paper 2008/25, United Nations World Institute for Development and Economic Research, New York.

Hochrainer, Stefan. 2009. "Assessing the Macroeconomic Impacts of Natural Disasters Are There Any?" Policy Research Working Paper 4968, World Bank, Washington, DC.

Ilzetzki, Ethan, Enrique G. Mendoza, and Carlos A. Vegh. 2013. "How Big (Small?) Are Fiscal Multipliers." *Journal of Monetary Economics* 60: 239–54.

Imam, Patrick. 2008. "Rapid Current Account Adjustments: Are Microstates Different?" IMF Working Paper WP/08/233, International Monetary Fund, Washington, DC.

———. 2010. "Exchange Rate Choices of Microstates" IMF Working Paper WP/10/12, International Monetary Fund, Washington, DC.

Jansen, Marion. 2004. "Income Volatility in Small and Developing Economies: Export Concentration Matters." WTO Discussion Paper number 3, World Trade Organization, Geneva.

Jansen, Marion, Carolina Lennon, and Roberta Piermartini. 2016. "Income Volatility: Whom You Trade with Matters." *Review of World Economics* 152: 127–46.

Kahneman, Daniel, and Amos Tversky. 1979. "Prospect Theory: An Analysis of Decision under Risk." *Econometrica* 47 (2) 263–91.

Klein, Michael, and Jay Shambaugh. 2006. "The Nature of Exchange Rate Regimes." NBER Working Paper 12729, National Bureau of Economic Research, Cambridge, MA.

Kouame, Auguste, and Ivanova Reyes. 2015. *Diversification of Markets: Degree of Synchronization of Caribbean Economies with the Business Cycle of Major Global Economies.* Washington, DC: World Bank.

Krugman, P. 1988. "Financing vs. Forgiving a Debt Overhang." *Journal of Development Economics* 29 (3): 253—68.

Lederman, Daniel, and William F. Maloney. 2012. *Does What You Export Matter? In Search of Empirical Guidance for Industrial Policies.* Latin American Development Series. Washington, DC: World Bank.

Melitz, Marc. 2003. "The Impact of Trade on Intra-Industry Reallocations and Aggregate Industry Productivity." *Econometrica* 71 (6): 1695–725.

Mendoza, Enrique. 1995. "The Terms of Trade, Real Exchange Rate, and Economic Fluctuations." *International Economic Review* 36 (1): 101–37.

———. 1997. "Terms-of-Trade Uncertainty and Economic Growth." *Journal of Development Economics* 54: 323–56.

Noy, Ilan. 2009. "The Macroeconomic Consequences of Disasters." *Journal of Development Economics* 88 (2): 221–31.

Ouattara, Bazoumana, and Eric Strobl. 2013. "The Fiscal Implications of Hurricane Strikes in the Caribbean." *Ecological Economics* 85 (C): 105–15.

Panizza, Ugo, and Andrea Presbitero. 2014. "Public Debt and Economic Growth: Is There a Causal Effect?" *Journal of Macroeconomics* 41: 21–41.

Pattillo, Catherine, Helene Poirson, and Luca Ricci. 2004. "What Are the Channels through Which External Debt Affects Growth?" IMF Working Paper 04/15, International Monetary Fund, Washington, DC.

Pritchett, Lant. 2000. "Understand Patterns of Economic Growth: Searching for Hills among Plateaus, Mountains, and Plains." *World Bank Economic Review* 14 (2): 221–50.

Raddatz, Claudio. 2007. "Are External Shocks Responsible for the Instability of Output in Low Income Countries?" *Journal of Development Economics* 84 (1): 155–87.

Ramey, Garey, and Ramey Valerie. 1995. "Cross-Country Evidence on the Link between Volatility and Growth." *The American Economic Review* 85 (5): 1138–51.

Rasmussen, Tobias. 2004. "Macroeconomic Implications of Natural Disasters in the Caribbean." IMF Working Paper 04/224, International Monetary Fund, Washington, DC.

Reinhart, Carmen, and Kenneth Rogoff. 2004. "The Modern History of Exchange Rate Arrangements: A Reinterpretation." *Quarterly Journal of Economics* 119 (1): 379–408.

Rodrik, Dani. 1998. "Why Do More Open Economies Have Bigger Governments?" *Journal of Political Economy* 106 (5): 997–1032.

Skidmore, Mark, and Hideki Toya. 2002. "Do Natural Disasters Promote Long Run Growth?" *Economic Inquiry* 40 (4): 664–87.

Strobl, Eric. 2012. "The Economic Growth Impact of Natural Disasters in Developing Countries: Evidence from Hurricane Strikes in the Central American and Caribbean Regions." *Journal of Development Economics* 97 (1): 130–41.

Turnovsky, Stephen, and Pradip Chattopadhyay. 2003. "Volatility and Growth in Developing Economies: Some Numerical Results and Empirical Evidence." *Journal of International Economics* 59 (2): 267–95.

CHAPTER 5

Open and Nimble: How Small Economies Adapt to Their Economic Challenges

The previous two chapters have highlighted the fact that while small economic size is not correlated directly with development outcomes, it does have implications for other economic outcomes that impact the development experience. Small economies tend to lack access to economies of scale and experience high levels of economic volatility while having high public debt levels and low savings. These are important empirical regularities to be aware of when crafting economic policy. Before discussing policy implications however, this chapter seeks to highlight the ways in which small economies have already adapted to this challenging economic environment, perhaps without even realizing it.

As the title of this book suggests, one important way small economies have adapted is by becoming open and nimble in their trading patterns. Open because small economies need the size of a global market in order to achieve economies of scale in production. Nimble because, without the ability to support a large number of industries in a given year, they need to achieve diversification of exports over time in order to reduce their risks to external economic volatility and terms of trade shocks. A second area of adaptation, though with some significant costs, is through patterns of migration and remittances. Emigrants abroad may provide a critical source of capital and economic support in the form of remittances during times of need, such as in response to natural disasters. However, such remittances may also distort the labor market in small economies.

Openness to Trade and Investment

As has been noted previously throughout this book (but not yet shown in the data), smaller economies tend to exhibit high levels of economic openness in terms of both trade and foreign direct investment (FDI) flows relative to gross domestic product (GDP). High levels of openness to trade may help a small economy's growth potential in a number of ways, including by providing a larger market for the goods they produce, opportunities for economies of scale, and transfers of technology that might not otherwise be developed. In other words, high levels of openness can serve to counteract some of the economic challenges small economies face which are laid out in the previous two chapters.

Figure 5.1 shows levels of trade openness in different groupings of countries around the world. From the distribution of openness across labor force size, it can be seen clearly that the level of trade openness declines significantly as countries increase in size, with a significant drop-off after reaching the median of the global distribution of working-age population. In addition, the distribution of openness across income levels shows that high-income, non-OECD countries are significantly more open when compared to other income groups. The high-income non-OECD group is also small relative to other income groups. This potentially supports the idea that high levels of openness may be related to minimizing any impact of small size on economic growth. Additionally, Caribbean countries exhibit substantially more openness to trade than the Latin American median, as well as the Central American median. This is likely related to Caribbean countries being both small in labor force and land mass. Small island economies often do not have the physical land or resources necessary to produce many goods and must rely more extensively on imports to fill their needs and export markets to achieve scale. Finally, the distribution of trade openness by economy type (ordered from smallest to largest) does not deviate significantly from what would be expected based on size effects alone.

Figure 5.1 Trade Openness, 1970–2013

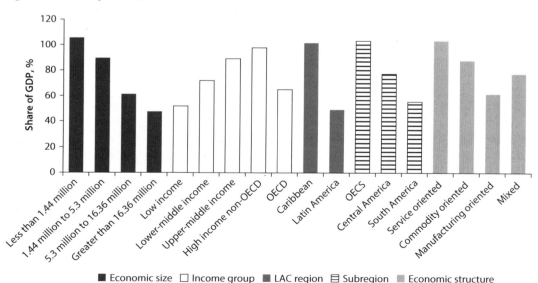

Source: Calculations based on data from World Bank World Development Indicators database.
Note: Bars in the figure represent the median value of average trade openness (exports + imports/GDP) from 1970 to 2013 among countries within each grouping.

In the economics literature, there is substantial evidence that openness to trade is positively correlated with economic growth and development. As mentioned earlier, Alesina, Spolaore, and Wacziarg (2005) find that openness has a significant positive relationship with growth, after controlling for several factors, including size, per capita income, government spending, and investment. Wacziarg and Welch (2008) find that over time, a country's openness to trade tends to increase with investment rates and growth. Frankel and Romer (1999) use geographic characteristics to create an instrument variable for trade openness uncorrelated with country income and find a significant positive relationship between their instrument and growth. Furthermore, they decompose growth into capital per worker, schooling, and productivity, finding that increased openness as measured by their instrument is associated with increases in all three of these components of growth. Lewer and Van den Berg (2003) survey the literature of estimates for trade's impact on economic growth. They find that, generally, a 1 percentage point increase in trade openness per year leads to about 0.2 percent GDP growth rate expansion per year, which is both statistically and economically significant. There seems to be a general consensus in the literature that openness to trade will likely have some positive impact on economic growth.

Another important component of openness is openness to foreign investment, and here the Caribbean in particular stands out. Figure 5.2 shows median FDI inflows over the last four decades for different groups of countries. The distribution of FDI flows across labor force size shows that FDI is greatest for small countries, as well as a negative relationship between size and FDI inflows.

Figure 5.2 Foreign Direct Investment Inflows, 1970–2013

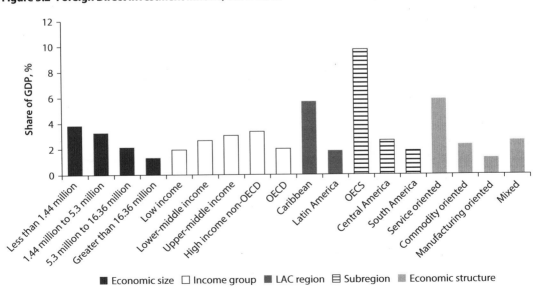

Source: Calculations based on data from World Bank World Development Indicators database.
Note: Bars in the figure represent the median value of average FDI inflows as a percentage of GDP from 1970 to 2013 among countries within each grouping.

Open and Nimble • http://dx.doi.org/10.1596/978-1-4648-1042-8

Even so, over the last 40 years Caribbean FDI inflows—especially to members of the Organisation of Eastern Caribbean States (OECS)—have dwarfed FDI to Latin America and other small economies. This is no coincidences, as countries in the Caribbean have been aggressive in courting FDI through tax breaks and other incentives, the merits of which are discussed further in chapter 6.[1] Additionally, figure 5.2 suggests a positive association between increasing income groups, aside from the OECD, and increasing FDI. Finally, the service-oriented economies in Latin America and the Caribbean (LAC) show high inflows of FDI, primarily because they tend to be Caribbean islands (which, as just mentioned, have been aggressively courting FDI).

There is evidence in the economics literature that FDI is positively correlated with growth, and that FDI can increase economic growth rates via technology transfers and linkages between foreign and domestic firms. For Lithuania, Javorcik (2004) finds evidence in firm-level data of positive spillovers between foreign-owned companies and local industry suppliers. In Indonesia, Blalock and Gertler (2008) find that domestic firms working in sectors that supply foreign entrants see productivity gains and lower prices, supporting the idea of growth-increasing knowledge transfers. Supporting these findings more broadly, Borensztein, De Gregorio, and Lee (1998) find that FDI produces more growth than domestic investment in a sample of 69 developing countries that meet a minimum standard of human capital development. This also suggests the positive role of technology transfers from foreign firms for growth, as long as workers in a country have the skill level to exploit such transfers.

However, Caribbean countries do not have outstanding long-run development levels, as might be expected based on the literature reviewed above and the region's exceptional FDI levels (see figures 2.4 and 5.2). As was discussed in chapter 3, small size appears related to the tendency of countries to form backward linkages with FDI. While FDI still provides capital which small economies may lack (see evidence on low savings rates in chapter 4), it is unclear whether the predicted benefits of backward linkages and spillovers can be fully obtained in small economies.

Nimbleness: Diversification Over Time

From the previous discussion in chapters 3 and 4, it may seem that small countries, due to their concentrated export sector, will struggle with terms of trade and growth volatility, given the association of export concentration with these variables The standard prescription given to countries experiencing high levels of external economic volatility is to diversify exports, but as discussed in chapter 3, small economies are unlikely to be able to do so in a meaningful way. However, small economies may have found another way: diversification over time.

A novel way to look at exports and diversification, in the context of historical exports, is proposed by Lederman, Pienknagura, and Rojas (2015) in a paper commissioned for this book. They propose a measure of "latent" diversification that captures all of the products that a country has exported in its history up to the current point in time. The authors argue that there are certain fixed costs that, once paid, make it easier to produce that product again in the future, even though a country may not have produced it actively for several years, and that this represents a potentially important and overlooked source of economic flexibility and diversification. In fact, they note that small economies tend to be the most dynamically diversified; that is, they both create and destroy the most product lines in a given year.

Figure 5.3 shows this dynamism at work. The figure illustrates the creation and destruction of products in a given year relative to the previous year, with countries classified by labor force size. The axes in each quadrant of the figure represent the global mean values of the creation and destruction of product lines, while the dots in each chart represent the average values during the period of years associated with it for those countries within the labor force grouping.

Observations farther to the right on a given plot indicate that a high percentage of products from the previous period are no longer produced relative to the

Figure 5.3 Creation and Destruction of Export Product Lines, 1972–2012

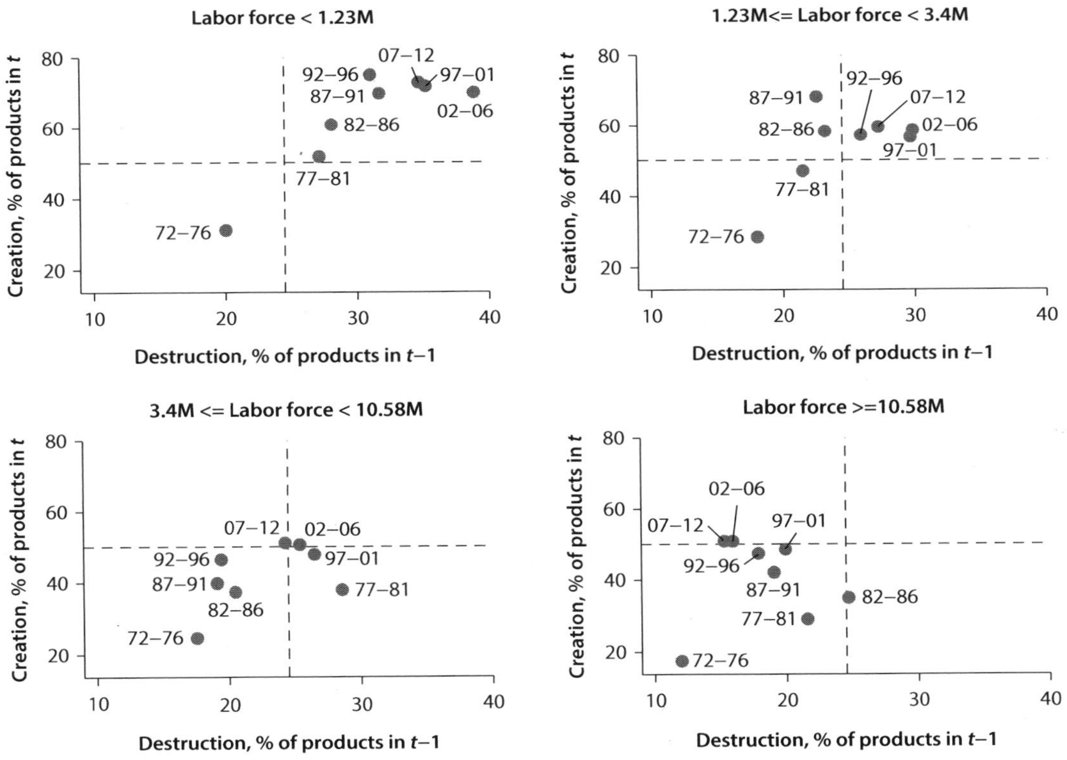

Sources: Calculations based on UN COMTRADE data and methods from Lederman, Pienknagura, and Rojas (2015).
Note: The figure shows average creation and destruction relative to *t*–1. The four plots represent countries grouped by labor force size. Moving up the y axis means creating new products in the current period that were not present in the previous period. Moving to the right on the x axis means that in the current period, production has stopped of more products from the previous period. The red lines represent the global mean values for the creation and destruction of products. This figure uses quartiles of the labor force with 1995 data.

world mean; observations further up the vertical axis on a given plot indicate a higher percentage of new export lines created in the current period relative to the world mean. The top two quadrants show that countries with a labor force size less than 3.4 million people tend to create and destroy many export product lines each period. The bottom two quadrants show that larger countries tend to export the same products that they produced in the previous period. The figure indicates that small economies tend to be more adaptable in response to changes in the global economic environment, which is consistent with the fact that they are highly open economies exposed to international economic conditions. In other words, they exhibit a high degree of nimbleness in their export sector.

In additional support of this point, figure 5.4 shows that small economies tend to have relatively large baskets of latent products relative to their export baskets in a given year. This implies that small economies are producing a fraction of the products that they have produced in the past during any given year. When taking into account that past production, these countries may have a much greater diversification of exports than is captured in traditional measures. As in figure 5.3, figure 5.4 shows that this impact is strongest in the smallest economies (represented by those with less than 1.44 million labor force size and the Caribbean islands in the figure), likely because of the additional factor of scarce land limiting contemporaneous production possibilities. From the

Figure 5.4 Ratio of Latent Products to Average Number of Export Lines, 1995–2013

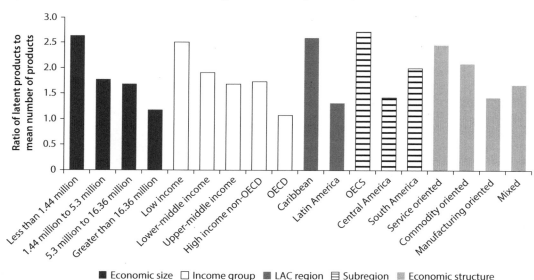

Sources: Calculations based on data from UN COMTRADE for trade in goods data and the World Bank's Consolidated Data on International Trade in Services v8.8.
Note: Bars are calculated as the ratio of the average number of latent products (in 2013) divided by the average number of exported products per year during the period 1995–2013. The bar represents the median value of this measure among countries within each grouping.

distribution over income groups, we can see that countries tend to have more of their historical trade lines open in a given year as they increase in income. This is likely because high-income countries tend to trade with more partners and have more stable trading relationships.

Lederman, Pienknagura, and Rojas (2015) find that their measure of latent diversification is correlated with lower terms of trade volatility and growth volatility.[2] As such, dynamic diversification over time could represent a very important way in which small economies are able to diversify their exports. It compensates for small economies' lack of labor market resources to produce a large basket of products contemporaneously, as well as the land shortages of small island economies. This nimbleness may be a significant factor in helping to reduce the high volatility of GDP and terms of trade growth rates that small economies face.

Emigration and Remittances

In addition to being open and nimble, small economies have another set of characteristics that may be a form of adaptation: high levels of migration and remittances. More emigrants abroad mean more capital inflows, in the form of remittances. This section discusses the implications of these facts for life in small economies.

Emigration Patterns

Figure 5.5 shows rates of emigration, measured as the ratio of the outstanding stock of emigrants relative to a country's labor force, for different groupings of countries. Looking at the ratio of emigrants to labor force size over country size groupings, it seems clear that small economies have a relatively higher number of emigrants abroad and that economic size is negatively related to emigration rates. Looking at the distribution of the emigrant-to-labor-force ratio over country income groupings, there does not appear to be a clear linear relationship between the two, but rather a quadratic one. This is a logical relationship if emigration is driven by returns to education and access to opportunity. It is likely that many individuals in low-income countries lack the resources to emigrate, while those in the OECD are already in relatively economically well off and stable countries with less incentive to migrate. Individuals in middle-income countries would appear to be prime candidates to migrate. This relationship is consistent with the United Nations' latest international migration report, which found that a clear majority of migrants (65 percent) are originally from middle-income countries (UN 2016). In the case of the LAC region, the Caribbean shows a high median emigrant-to-labor-force ratio relative to the LAC median; the OECS countries show a higher median ratio than the rest of the LAC small economies. This is likely because Caribbean and OECS economies are among the smallest in the region (see figure 2.3), which would increase the ratio of emigrants to labor force.

Figure 5.5 Stock of Emigrants over Labor Force, 2015

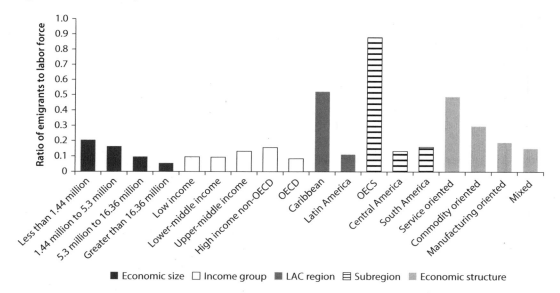

Sources: Calculations based on data from the UN Department of Economic and Social Affairs Migrant Stock data set and World Bank World Development Indicators database.

Note: The figure represents the ratio of the emigrant stock in 2015 from a given country over the 2013 labor force in that country. The bars represent the median value of this ratio for a given grouping of countries.

Finally, looking at the distribution of the emigrant-to-labor-force ratio by export structure, we see that service-oriented and commodity-export-oriented economies have a higher ratio value. This again is likely because they tend to be made up of significantly smaller countries in the Caribbean.

What factors explain these high levels of emigration in small economies? Table 5.1 attempts to shed light on this difficult question. One common hypothesis is that migrants leave their home country in search of economic opportunities. Column 1 tests this hypothesis using the domestic unemployment rate as a proxy for labor market conditions. The results confirm the discussion above, namely, that emigration rates appear to be related negatively to economic size and in a nonlinear fashion with development levels. However, the coefficient on unemployment is not statistically significant.

Another way to think about this hypothesis is in terms of variety of opportunities. Perhaps people migrate not because there are no jobs in their country, but rather because their country is highly specialized in sectors for which they do not want to work. Column 2 tests this idea by including the number of different exported products as a proxy for variety of opportunities. The coefficient on this term is statistically significant, but with the opposite sign of that predicted by the theory outlined above.

A final idea is that it may be the case that being open to trade and having economic relations with a particular destination may lead that country to be more open to your emigrants. Column 3 finds a positive and weakly significant

Table 5.1 Determinants of Emigrant Ratio

Variable	(1) Emigrant ratio	(2) Emigrant ratio	(3) Emigrant ratio	(4) Emigrant ratio
Working-age population	−0.315***	−0.413***	−0.408***	−0.415***
	(0.0448)	(0.0488)	(0.0561)	(0.0560)
GDP per capita PPP	4.092***	3.817***	4.002***	3.824***
	(0.951)	(0.930)	(0.922)	(0.931)
GDP per capita PPP squared	−0.223***	−0.217***	−0.225***	−0.217***
	(0.0522)	(0.0502)	(0.0499)	(0.0502)
Unemployment rate	0.0982	0.0737	0.0774	0.0734
	(0.119)	(0.117)	(0.117)	(0.117)
Number of export products		0.504**		0.479
		(0.220)		(0.346)
Number of trading partners			0.662*	0.0488
			(0.353)	(0.556)
Constant	−20.11***	−20.97***	−21.97***	−21.07***
	(4.126)	(3.929)	(3.976)	(4.023)
Observations	155	155	155	155
R-squared	0.371	0.390	0.383	0.390

Sources: Calculations based on data from World Bank World Development Indicators database, UN COMMTRADE, Consolidated data on Trade in Services v8.8, and the UN Department of Economic and Social Affairs Migrant Stock data set.
Note: All variables are in logs. Robust standard errors in parentheses. PPP = purchasing power parity.
***$p<0.01$; **$p<0.05$; *$p<0.1$.

relationship between the number of destination markets and emigration rates. However, when including both products and partners in column 4, both lose statistically significance. In short, from our data one thing is clear: economic size is negatively correlated with emigration rates. Why that might be and if there are particular channels other than size itself which lead to higher emigration rates is an interesting and important question for further research.

Evidence in the economics literature on how emigration relates to growth outcomes is mixed. One widely discussed implication for economic growth from high emigration levels is the idea of a "brain drain." It is commonly recognized that migrants are not an unbiased sample of people from their host country and specifically that migrants tend to be more educated than those they leave behind.[3] Theorists have noted that this might reduce a country's growth potential through a reduction in average human capital in the sending country (Grubel and Scott 1966; Bhagwati and Hamada 1974; Kwok and Leland 1982). However, others argue that greater returns to education among migrants may encourage investment in education in the sending country. The argument is that when migration is not certain to occur but higher returns abroad encourage investment in education, a country allowing emigration may end up with a net gain in the average education level of those residents that stay (Mountford 1997). Beine, Docquier, and Rapoport (2008) test this idea using a data set with migration and education data for 127 countries. They find that a doubling of the emigration rate results in about a 5 percent increase in human capital formation in a given country's population (including the emigrants).

When the emigrants are netted out there are countries, typically those with lower levels of human capital and lower rates of migration of skilled workers, that seem to have experienced this beneficial brain drain effect. Thus, high levels of skilled worker emigration may not always reduce growth potential.

Another potential impact of emigration on growth may come through the channel of increased trade and financial flows to the sending country. Gould (1994) finds that in the case of the United States, larger stocks of migrants within the U.S. from a given country are associated with increased trade between the United States and that country. He postulates this is because immigrants bring with them important business contacts, language skills, and local market knowledge. In the case of the United States, Javorcik et al. (2011) present evidence that U.S. FDI flows are correlated positively with the presence of migrants from the FDI receiving country in the United States. These authors use a data set of 56 countries and through instrument variable regression find that a 1 percent increase in the migrant stock results in a 0.35–0.42 percentage point increase in the FDI stock. Additionally, Niimi and Ozden (2006) find, using instrumental variable regressions, that having more emigrants abroad and being smaller are associated with higher levels of remittance receipts.

Thus, while it is unclear whether emigration itself impacts growth potential, it does seem to be associated with increased openness to trade and investment as well as remittances. Having discussed the impacts of openness in the previous section of this chapter, the next section discusses the role remittances play in small economies.

Remittances: Positive or Negative?

Another way in which small economies might effectively increase their savings is through high levels of remittances. To the extent that small countries receive a disproportionately high level of remittances, these funds may function as a substitute for domestic savings or have other growth-enhancing effects and volatility reducing effects, a possibility explored in this section.

Table 5.2 shows the results of a regression analysis for the determinants of remittances. Column 1 shows that smaller economies tend to have higher levels of remittances as a share of GDP. Column 2 shows that remittances are negatively related to development. Column 3 shows that when the emigrant-to-labor-force ratio is included, labor force loses significance, which is supportive of the idea that remittances are mainly driven by the number of emigrants abroad as opposed to a direct effect of being small. Having more migrants abroad relative to the labor force is associated with higher levels of remittances relative to GDP. Column 4 includes unemployment, which is positively correlated with remittances; however, the direction of causality is not clear. This may be a good thing, to the extent that it indicates remittances are countercyclical and are used as a form of unemployment insurance

Table 5.2 Determinants of Remittances

Variable	(1) Remittances/GDP	(2) Remittances/GDP	(3) Remittances/GDP	(4) Remittances/GDP
Working-age population	−0.249***	−0.251***	0.00168	0.0315
	(0.0586)	(0.0490)	(0.0550)	(0.0597)
GDP per capita PPP		−0.559***	−0.654***	−0.667***
		(0.114)	(0.107)	(0.106)
Emigrant ratio			0.800***	0.758***
			(0.103)	(0.101)
Unemployment rate				0.425**
				(0.167)
Constant	0.750***	5.861***	8.187***	7.293***
	(0.154)	(1.051)	(1.044)	(1.023)
Observations	158	158	158	158
R-squared	0.079	0.233	0.438	0.474

Source: Calculations based on data from World Bank World Development Indicators database, and the UN Department of Economic and Social Affairs Migrant Stock data set.
Note: All variables are in logs. Robust standard errors in parentheses. PPP = purchasing power parity.
***$p<0.01$, **$p<0.05$, *$p<0.1$.

by individuals, but it could also indicate that remittances are a distortion in the labor market (discussed further below).

Results in the economic literature on the relationship between remittances and growth are mixed. Many cross-sectional studies have found conditional evidence that remittances are positively related to growth. Giuliano and Ruiz-Arranz (2009) find a positive relationship between remittances and growth, and that this relationship is strongest for countries with less-developed financial sectors. These findings indicate that remittances may increase growth by improving access to credit and entrepreneurship opportunities. Catrinescu et al. (2009) argue that remittances are more likely to contribute to economic growth in the presence of higher-quality political and economic institutions because these help facilitate increased investment activities. The results of their dynamic panel data analysis show that remittances are positively correlated with growth in most cases when taking into account institutional factors. Furthermore, Adams and Page (2005) find that remittances may play a role in reducing poverty. According to their estimates, a 10 percent increase in remittances per capita will lead to a 3.5 percent reduction in the share of people living in poverty. Acosta, Fajnzylber, and Lopez (2008) also find evidence that remittances decrease poverty by increasing GDP per capita, and that most of this increase in GDP per capita comes from increased domestic investment.

Others take a more negative view. Chami, Fullenkamp, and Jahjah (2005) argue that remittances induce an important moral hazard problem, which could take the specific form of reduced labor market participation by individuals receiving remittances. These authors find in a panel estimation of 113 countries that remittances are negatively related to economic growth. Acosta, Fajnzylber, and Lopez (2008) analyze household survey data in 11 LAC countries.

They find some evidence that remittances decrease hours worked and labor force participation rate, consistent with the idea that remittances have an adverse effect on the labor market. Using household survey data, Hanson (2007) and Kim (2007) corroborate these results in the cases of Mexico and Jamaica, respectively. However, Posso (2012) analyzes a panel of 67 countries and finds that remittances have a positive impact on labor force participation. He theorizes this is because remittances are associated with increased credit generation, resulting in job creation.

Table 5.3 further evaluates the potential labor market impact of remittances. It shows the results of regression analysis on the determinants of the long-run average unemployment rate in our data set. Column 1 shows that being small appears to have a negative correlation with unemployment. The unemployment rate is a ratio of unemployed persons to the labor force and thus might be mechanically correlated with the labor force. Therefore, we also report the results of an *F*-test in which the coefficient on labor force is different from negative 1 (see the last row of table 5.3). This is equivalent to testing whether or not the labor force size has an impact on unemployed persons. In fact, the test results imply that labor force size is positively related to the unemployment rate, because the estimated coefficient is significantly greater than −1. Column 4 shows that the ratio of emigrants to working-age population is also positively correlated with unemployment.

Table 5.3 Unemployment and Remittances

Variable	(1) Unemployment rate	(2) Unemployment rate	(3) Unemployment rate	(4) Unemployment rate
Working-age population	−0.0460* (0.0270)	−0.0465* (0.0274)	−0.0361 (0.0291)	−0.000417 (0.0355)
GDP per capita PPP		0.0362 (0.0530)	0.0618 (0.0543)	0.0283 (0.0574)
Remittances/GDP			0.0545 (0.0345)	0.00905 (0.0390)
Emigrant ratio				0.153** (0.0659)
Constant	−2.266*** (0.436)	−2.589*** (0.556)	−2.994*** (0.620)	−2.860*** (0.601)
Observations	156	156	156	156
R-squared	0.014	0.018	0.036	0.076
Test	fstat = 1247.97	fstat = 1209.79	fstat = 1097.75	fstat = 793.82
Test if B on log(average working-age population) = −1	pval = 0.00	pval = 0.00	pval = 0.00	pval = 0.00

Sources: Calculations based on data from World Bank World Development Indicators database, and the UN Department of Economic and Social Affairs Migrant Stock data set.

Note: All variables are in logs. The regression log(unemployed person/labor force) = B*log(labor force) + error can be rewritten as log(unemployed persons) = (B + 1) log(laborforce) + error. Testing whether the estimated B = −1 is equivalent to the test of B + 1 = 0. The unemployment rate was calculated with respect to working-age population (as opposed to labor force) to match the independent variable representing size. Both are averages for the period 1990–2013.

Robust standard errors in parentheses. PPP = purchasing power parity.

***p<0.01, **p<0.05, *p<0.1

Table 5.4 Remittances and Participation

Variable	(1) log(participation rate)	(2) log(participation rate)	(3) log(participation rate)	(4) log(participation rate)
Working-age population	0.00308 (0.00625)	0.00353 (0.00643)	−0.00173 (0.00655)	−0.000723 (0.00734)
GDP per capita PPP		−0.0115 (0.0101)	−0.0229** (0.00963)	−0.0239** (0.0106)
Remittances/GDP			−0.0240*** (0.00716)	−0.0253*** (0.00838)
Emigrant ratio				0.00424 (0.0136)
Constant	4.160*** (0.0944)	4.258*** (0.123)	4.448*** (0.128)	4.452*** (0.130)
Observations	163	163	163	163
R-squared	0.001	0.010	0.071	0.072
Test	fstat = 25756.14	fstat = 24360.61	fstat = 23196.97	fstat = 18546.78
Test if B on log(average working-age population) = −1	pval = 0.00	pval = 0.00	pval = 0.00	pval = 0.00

Sources: Calculations based on data from World Bank World Development Indicators database, and the UN Department of Economic and Social Affairs Migrant Stock data set.

Note: All variables are in logs. The regression ln(labor force/working-age population) = B*ln(working-age population) + e can be rewritten as ln(labor force) = (b + 1)*ln(working-age population) + e. Testing whether the estimated B = − 1 is equivalent to the test of B + 1 = 0. Both are averages from 1990–2013.

Robust standard errors in parentheses. PPP = purchasing power parity.

***p<0.01, **p<0.05, *p<0.1

Table 5.4 shows the results of a similar set of regressions on the participation rate. As discussed above, there may be a mechanical negative correlation between working-age population and the participation rate, so we report the results of an *F*-test testing whether the coefficient on working-age population is different from −1. The results again imply that size has a positive impact on the participation rate because the estimated coefficient is significantly greater than −1. Columns 3 and 4 show that development and remittances are both negatively related to participation. This implies lower participation in the labor force for countries with higher remittances, which would include many small economies. Thus, we find evidence in our data consistent with the literature showing that remittances may have negative labor market impacts.

In addition to potential impacts on growth and the creation of moral hazard in the labor market, remittances may have important impacts, both positive and negative, on volatility as well as other variables. In terms of managing volatility, evidence suggests that remittances tend to be countercyclical to the receiving country and therefore can help recipient economies deal with economic volatility (see Kapur 2004; World Bank 2006; Frankel 2011). However, Barajas et al. (2012) find that remittances constitute an important and overlooked form of openness to the global economic environment, and that external shocks from abroad may be passed to the receiving economy through reduced remittances. In fact, they find that it is significantly more likely for a downturn in a remittance-sending country to result in reduced remittance outflows than the reverse case. This suggests that remittances may have an asymmetric effect on volatility exposure and increase the pass-through of downward risks. Other authors—such as Mohapatra, Joseph, and Ratha (2009)—find that remittances tend to increase during natural disasters, suggesting that they may provide some form of disaster risk insurance in countries that receive them. Additionally, Yang (2008) analyzes data on hurricane strikes and resultant international flows in 87 countries. He finds that countries in the poorer half of the sample were more likely to receive significant increases in remittance flows after a strike.

In summary, then, although remittances may be associated with positive growth and poverty reduction outcomes, the research results are mixed. There is some evidence that remittances may be associated with negative labor market outcomes, and although they tend to be countercyclical, they might at the same time increase exposure to external volatility. Therefore, it is not clear that placing a policy emphasis on remittances is a solution to the economic challenges small economies face.

Notes

1. For more detailed analysis of FDI trends and policy in the Caribbean, see ECLAC (2015) and de Groot and Pérez Ludeña (2014).

2. More traditional measures of diversification are also correlated with lower terms of trade volatility and growth volatility, a point discussed chapters 3 and 4.

3. See Carrington and Detragiache (1998) for evidence that immigrants in the United States tend to be more educated than those they left behind.

References

Acosta, Pablo, Pablo Fajnzylber, and Humberto Lopez. 2008. "Remittances and Household Behavior." In *Remittances and Development Lessons from Latin America*, edited by Pablo Fajnzylber and J. Humberto López, 133–71. Washington, DC: World Bank.

Adams, Richard, and John Page. 2005. "Do International Migration and Remittances Reduce Poverty in Developing Countries?" *World Development* 33 (10): 1645–99.

Alesina, Alberto, Enrico Spolaore, and Romain Wacziarg. 2005. "Trade, Growth, and the Size of Countries." In *Handbook of Economic Growth*, edited by P. Aghion and S. Durlauf. Amsterdam: North Holland.

Barajas, Adolfo, Ralph Chami, Christian Ebeke, and Sampawende J. A. Tapsoba. 2012. "Worker's Remittances: An Overlooked Channel of International Business Cycle Transmission?" IMF Working Paper WP/12/251, International Monetary Fund, Washington, DC.

Beine, Michel, Frederic Docquier, and Hillel Rapoport. 2008. "Brain Drain and Human Capital Formation in Developing Countries: Winners and Losers." *Economic Journal* 118 (528): 631–52.

Bhagwati, Jagdish, and Koichi Hamada. 1974. "The Brain Drain, International Integration of Markets for Professionals and Unemployment: A Theoretical Analysis." *Journal of Development Economics* 1 (1): 19–42.

Blalock, Garrick, and Paul Gertler. 2008. "Welfare Gains from Foreign Direct Investment through Technology Transfer to Local Suppliers." *Journal of International Economics* 74 (2): 402–21.

Borensztein, Eduardo, Jose De Gregorio, and Jong-Wha Lee. 1998. "How Does Foreign Direct Investment Affect Economic Growth?" *Journal of International Economics* 45 (1): 115–35.

Carrington, William, and Enrica Detragiache. 1998. "How Big Is the Brain Drain?" IMF Working Paper 98/102, International Monetary Fund, Washington, DC.

Catrinescu, Natalia, Miguel Leon-Ledesma, Matloob Piracha, and Bryce Quillin. 2009. "Remittances, Institutions, and Economic Growth." *World Development* 37 (1): 81–92.

Chami, Ralph, Connel Fullenkamp, and Samir Jahjah. 2005. "Are Immigrant Remittance Flows a Source of Capital for Development?" *IMF Staff Papers* 52 (1): 55–81.

De Groot, Olaf, and Miguel Pérez Ludeña. 2014. "Foreign Direct Investment in the Caribbean: Trends, Determinants, and Policies." Studies and Perspectives 35, ECLAC, United Nations. http://repositorio.cepal.org/bitstream/handle/11362/36620/1/S2014046_en.pdf.

ECLAC (Economic Commission for Latin America and the Caribbean). 2015. *Foreign Direct Investment in Latin America and the Caribbean*. Santiago: ECLAC, United Nations.

Frankel, Jeffrey. 2011. "Are Bilateral Remittances Countercyclical?" *Open Economies Review* 22 (1): 1–16.

Frankel, Jeffrey, and David Romer. 1999. "Does Trade Cause Growth?" *American Economic Review* 89 (3): 379–99.

Giuliano, Paola, and Marta Ruiz-Arranz. 2009. "Remittances, Financial Development, and Growth." *Journal of Development Economics* 90 (1): 144–52.

Gould, David M. 1994. "Immigrant Links to the Home Country: Empirical Implications for U.S. Bilateral Trade Flows." *Review of Economics and Statistics* 76: 302–16.

Grubel, Herbert B., and Anthony D. Scott. 1966. "The International Flow of Human Capital." *American Economic Review* 56: 268–74.

Hanson, Gordon. 2007. "Emigration, Remittances, and Labor Force Participation in Mexico." INTAL-ITD Working Paper 28, Inter-American Development Bank, Washington, DC.

Javorcik, B. S. 2004. "Does Foreign Direct Investment Increase the Productivity of Domestic Firms? In Search of Spillovers through Backward Linkages." *American Economic Review* 94 (3): 605–27.

Javorcik, Beata, Caglar Olzden, Mariana Spatareanu, and Cristina Neagu. 2011. "Migrant Networks and Foreign Direct Investment." *Journal of Development Economics* 94 (2): 231–41.

Kapur, Devesh. 2004. "'Remittances': The New Development Mantra?" G24 Discussion Paper 29, United Nations Conference on Trade and Development, Geneva.

Kim, Namsuk. 2007. "The Impact of Remittances on Labor Supply: The Case of Jamaica." Research Working Paper 4120, World Bank, Washington, DC.

Kwok, Viem, and Hayne Leland. 1982. "An Economic Model of the Brain Drain." *American Economic Review* 72 (1): 91–100.

Lederman, Daniel, Samuel Pienknagura, and Diego Rojas. 2015. "Latent Trade Diversification and Its Relevance for Macroeconomic Stability." Working Paper 7332, World Bank, Washington, DC.

Lewer, Joshua, and Hendrik Van den Berg. 2003. "How Large Is International Trade's Effect on Economic Growth?" *Journal of Economic Surveys* 17 (3): 363–96.

Mohapatra, Sanket, George Joseph, and Dilip Ratha. 2009. "Remittances and Natural Disasters Ex-Post Response and Contribution to Ex-Ante Preparedness." Policy Research Working Paper 4972, World Bank, Washington, DC.

Mountford, Andrew. 1997. "Can Brain Drain Be Good for Growth in the Source Economy?" *Journal of Development Economics* 53 (2): 287–303.

Niimi, Yoko, and Caglar Ozden. 2006. "Migration and Remittances: Causes and Linkages." Policy Research Working Paper 4087, World Bank, Washington, DC.

Posso, Alberto. 2012. "Remittances and Aggregate Labor Supply: Evidence from Sixty-Six Developing Nations." *Developing Economies* 50 (1): 25–39.

Wacziarg, Romain, and Karen Welch. 2008. "Trade Liberalization and Growth: New Evidence." *World Bank Economic Review* 22 (2): 187–231.

World Bank. 2006. "Economic Implications of Remittances and Migration." Global Economic Prospects Series, World Bank, Washington, DC.

Yang, Dean. 2008. "Coping with Disaster: The Impact of Hurricanes on International Financial Flows, 1970–2002." *B.E. Journal of Economic Analysis & Policy* 8 (1): 1–45.

UN (United Nations). 2016. *International Migration Report 2015: Highlights* (ST/ESA/SER.A/375), Department of Economic and Social Affairs, Population Division, UN, New York.

CHAPTER 6

Policy Implications

The previous chapters clearly show that small economies face certain unique economic challenges relative to larger economies. However, it is also clear that size is not destiny; when it comes to economic outcomes, these challenges can be overcome. Armed with the understanding of size and its relationship with particular economic outcomes outlined in this book, several policy priorities emerge which can help small economies in Latin America and the Caribbean (LAC) and elsewhere achieve a more stable growth path.

Economic Characteristics of Small Economies

The most important characteristic of small economies is that they can and often do grow fast and reach high levels of development. That being said, while these economies do not face lower growth potential, they do face a number of economic challenges which may require different strategies to achieve development.

A fundamental difference between small and large economies is their inability to access economies of scale. This shows up in the fact that small economies tend to have highly specialized export structures and tend not to be competitive, exporting many goods that exhibit increasing returns to scale. A lack of scale economies may also have a dampening effect on the benefits of FDI by limiting the positive spillover effects resulting from interaction between foreign and domestic firms. Finally, scale also appears to be a factor in government spending patterns, with small economies showing relatively high costs of government relative to GDP. This lack of access to economies of scale and resulting characteristics have a number of important economic implications.

The first economic implication is increased economic volatility. The concentration of exports into a small number of products and destination markets leads small economies to exhibit high terms of trade growth volatility. This in turn tends to make GDP growth more volatile, and this relationship is amplified by the fact that small economies are very open to trade, with high levels of trade relative to GDP. Small economies also exhibit high concentration in terms of the number of export markets, and there is some emerging evidence that this may be related to increased growth volatility, as shocks in trading partner countries impact the home market. The effect of this channel on volatility would again be amplified in highly open economies.

An additional contributor to high levels of uncertainty and growth volatility in small economies, and particularly small island economies such as those in the Caribbean, is the fact that these economies face high relative costs of natural disasters. Small economies are not necessarily more prone to such events; however, they experience disproportionately large impacts from them. While large countries can maintain internal risk-sharing arrangements and are unlikely to be crippled by a disaster, small economies often see large chunks of their population/territory impacted by disaster events. Aside from the cost in human lives, these events have large financial costs and economic impacts in small economies.

This volatility and higher relative costs of natural disasters feed into a second economic challenge that small economies face: managing public debt. Smaller economies tend to spend relatively more on their governments, one reason for which is their inability to exploit economies of scale in the provision of public goods. In addition to this tendency for government services to be more costly on a per capita basis in small economies, LAC small economies exhibit poor government revenue generation as a share of GDP. These facts come together with large damages from natural disasters, which impact growth rate volatility and necessitate expensive reconstruction efforts, to create an environment favorable to the buildup of persistently high levels of public debt.

The external sources of uncertainty noted in the preceding section and the high levels of debt in small economies create an environment supportive of persistently low levels of domestic savings, which may hurt long-run growth potential. High debt levels due to relatively more-costly government, lower government revenue generation (in LAC), and natural disaster–induced borrowing imply low levels of public savings. Uncertainty related to terms of trade volatility, growth rate volatility, and climate events combine to increase shortsighted behavior in private actors, resulting in lower than optimal private savings rates. Lower levels of domestic savings are related to lower levels of investment and slower growth over the long run.

In light of these challenging economic conditions, small economies have adapted. Small economies tend to be highly open to trade and foreign investment, which may help them gain economies of scale by producing for larger markets and increase their levels of investment. They are also nimble in what they export, opening and closing new product lines more quickly than larger economies. This may help reduce economic volatility from terms of trade growth shocks. However, these adaptations are not enough, and more can be done. Given the understanding laid out above, there are specific policy priorities that can help address the unique challenges small economies face.

Policy Solutions

This book emphasizes the idea that size matters for development outcomes, but also that size is not necessarily a determinative factor. A better understanding of challenges to growth in small economies suggests that almost all of these challenges can be minimized with an appropriate policy response. Broadly speaking, what emerges from this book is the need to focus the policy dialogue in small economies in LAC and worldwide on four key areas: (1) addressing external economic vulnerability, (2) addressing natural disaster risks, (3) addressing diseconomies of scale in government, and (4) tax system reforms. The following discussion of broad policy areas is framed in the context of LAC small economies, but the need to address these policy areas is of relevance to small economies worldwide.

Addressing Economic Volatility through Diversification

There is unfortunately no way to eliminate economic volatility completely. High levels of economic integration and its inherent international exposure are a necessary fact of life for small economies in LAC and worldwide. Additionally, being a small island state with limited land and resources imposes physical restraints on a country's ability to protect against trade risks through diversifying its contemporaneous export basket. Nevertheless, it may still be possible to reduce external volatility risk from openness by diversifying over time and developing latent diversification. In fact, small countries already seem to exhibit a natural tendency toward this dynamism. Research shows that small economies are changing products in their export basket more frequently than large economies from year to year. This ability to rapidly change export products in response to changing global economic conditions is an important form of diversification for small economies. Governments could augment this flexibility in the export sector by encouraging new export ventures and ventures into nontraditional product lines. Small economies may also be able to expand the number of export markets to which they cater in order to reduce the volatility associated with being highly open. A country can make efforts to expand the number of export products it produces over time and to increase the number of destination markets with which it trades at the same time. In achieving this goal for LAC, further regional integration and harmonization of product standards are potentially helpful. Regional integration can strengthen countries' position in trade agreement negotiations and make the region a more desirable trading partner to the rest of the world. Aside from aiding in the process of opening new export markets, further regional integration in a broader sense has tremendous value for the region in addressing natural disaster risk and helping achieve better fiscal balances.

The case of Mauritius highlights the principle that economic flexibility in small economies can mitigate external volatility. Commonly referred to as a growth miracle, the small island country of Mauritius experienced real GDP growth between 1977 and 2006 of 5.2 percent per year, compared with 3.3 percent in the rest of Africa. It grew this fast while simultaneously transitioning from an economy dependent upon agriculture to one with a large share of manufacturing and services (Subramanian 2009). Although there is some disagreement about the fundamental causes of this growth, the last 30 years of Mauritian history reveal that economic flexibility and openness played an important part in the story behind this growth miracle.

One of the key instigators of growth was the establishment of export processing zones in the 1980s (Rodrik 1998). Throughout the 1980s, the Mauritian economy was mainly driven by sugar production, which left the economy vulnerable to external commodity price shocks. This led the government to push for export processing zones in an attempt to diversify the economy. Key features of these zones included tax incentives for exporting firms and reduced duties on inputs to exporting industries not locally available. By the end of the 1980s, the export processing zones employed more people than the agricultural sector. The zones led to preferential trade policies with the EU, to a booming Mauritian textile industry, and to large amounts of foreign investment and knowledge coming into the country (Zafar 2011).

In the mid-2000s, Mauritius again faced external threats. Textile trade preferences with the European Union that had helped support the textile industry expired, and the 2008 financial crisis and subsequent decline in global trade growth was another shock. The government responded by instituting a reform program in 2006 aimed at reducing regulatory barriers to forming businesses, lowering taxes, and making it easier for immigrants to become citizens. The government also implemented key banking reforms aimed at providing financing to small business. This resulted in the country climbing in rankings of business climate and furthered its transition to a service-based economy driven by tourism and the financial sector (Frankel 2010).

While other factors such as institutions may have played a role, this history of transformation shows that openness, flexibility, and diversification over time in the Mauritian economy contributed to sustaining growth. The government has both encouraged diversification into new sectors where necessary, and has also aimed to reduce regulations and provide resources and skills for individuals and companies to innovate in the face of a challenging economic environment.

Addressing Disaster Risk through Risk Pooling and Self-Insurance

There are two elements that countries should consider when thinking about policies to reduce the impact of natural disasters: preparation and financing the recovery. Both of these can be helped by increased regional integration, in the case of the Caribbean. In terms of preparation, governments must continue to pool resources and fund region-wide research and forecasting initiatives that seek to understand natural disasters and the specific vulnerabilities of countries in the region. The hope is that with more advanced and even country-specific warning and prediction capabilities, losses can be minimized. An additional aspect of preparation is ensuring that all infrastructure and public goods are modernized and built as disaster resistant as possible. It has often been noted that the upfront costs of improving buildings and infrastructure are lower than replacement costs (Charveriat 2000). Public infrastructure systems should be upgraded and kept up to date where possible, to avoid outages and destruction, as well as minimize repair costs in the event of a disaster.

A second disaster recovery issue is preparing to finance the reconstruction effort. In an ideal world, governments in the region would insure themselves fully against the risk of natural disasters. Unfortunately, natural disasters present several problems for private insurance markets. It is difficult for insurance companies to reliably assess disaster risk, due to the unpredictability of weather events. There is also a large adverse selection problem in that most people and countries buying disaster insurance are located in disaster-prone areas, and therefore the pool of purchasers is small and highly vulnerable.

One potential solution to this issue is more regional risk pooling initiatives such as the Caribbean Catastrophe Risk Insurance Facility. Formed in 2007 with the help of international institutions, the facility offers insurance for earthquakes, cyclones, and excessive rainfall events. The facility functions much like traditional insurance; it collects premiums from countries based on their likely disaster risk and then spreads the risk to others using financial instruments. The facility has made 21 payouts with a total value of US$68 million. In 2014 the organization expanded to offer insurance products to some Central American countries.

Pooling risk through such initiatives as the Caribbean Catastrophe Risk Insurance Facility is an important part of risk management for small and vulnerable countries, but it may not be enough. In the case of the facility, most member countries are vulnerable to natural disasters, and thus the adverse selection problem remains. This system could potentially work better if non-Caribbean countries that are less vulnerable to disasters and/or are located in a different region of the world with different disaster risks can be convinced to join. Nevertheless, regional risk pooling is better than no risk pooling.

Relatedly, small economies should establish mechanisms for raising public savings and addressing the issue of high public debt in order to enable the buildup of resources for responding to disasters. It is important for these economies to try to maintain primary balance surpluses, particularly in good economic times. These savings will provide an important form of self-insurance against future natural disasters and limit the growth of public debt levels. As noted in the discussion on public debt in chapter 4, debt growth in the Caribbean over the last 20 years has been mainly due to interest payments on pre-existing debt and the assumption of contingent liabilities by central governments. In addressing the second point, stricter regulation and greater transparency regarding the administration of government enterprises and public–private partnerships may help resolve some of these issues before they become crises. Moreover, governments could alter their accounting practices to explicitly account for their contingent liabilities and provide clearer definitions of when the government will step in and how much help they will provide in order to reduce the potential for moral hazard.[1]

Open and Nimble • http://dx.doi.org/10.1596/978-1-4648-1042-8

Addressing Fiscal Challenges through Regional Integration Efforts and Innovation in Government

As discussed throughout this book, small economies often have higher relative costs of governance due to diseconomies of scale in the provision of public goods and limited resources. Small island economies may also have issues providing public services to their population located on outlying islands far away from main population centers. These issues can potentially be addressed through regional integration efforts and innovation in the provision of public services.

Further regional integration can help offset problems related to government fiscal balances by allowing for cost pooling in government services. A natural opportunity for regional integration in the provision of public services is joint investments in transportation infrastructure in order to better connect economies in LAC, particularly those in the Caribbean. More connections between islands would benefit everyone, but transportation infrastructure is expensive; regional cost pooling would make this more feasible. Other areas that may see similar benefits from greater economies of scale associated with regional integration are public utilities and electricity generation. These are commonly thought to be subject to increasing returns to scale and require large fixed investments that small economies may not be able to carry out on their own.

A prominent example of regional integration efforts aimed at achieving scale in the provision of public goods is the recent development of an integrated electric system in Central America. Originally begun in 1987 and formalized in the Marco treaty signed in 1996, these efforts consisted of the development of a transmission line (known as the SIEPAC line) that can send power from Guatemala to Panama, a regional electric market (MER), and a regional electric regulatory agency (EOR), all of which are now operational. The electric system is run by a consortium of transmission operators from the six host countries (Economic Consulting Associates 2010).

Thorough evaluations of the actual performance of the regional grid do not yet appear to exist. Nevertheless, in theory Central American countries should see benefits from electric market integration both in terms of increasing scale in electricity generation and reducing exposure to external volatility. Electricity generation is typically thought of as subject to increasing returns to scale, particularly at low levels of output, meaning that average costs decline as companies become larger (Christensen and Greene 1976). In the context of small economies with small domestic markets, regional integration in this sector that creates a larger electric market may result in lower generation costs. Regarding benefits to managing external volatility, the system may help the region become less dependent upon energy imports and international oil prices. Previous work has shown that Central America imports a great deal of oil-based energy but has a large potential for exploiting renewables (Dolezal et al. 2013). To the extent that the interconnected grid allows for further development of renewable resources in Central America, countries will be less vulnerable to international oil price shocks (Yepez-Garcia and Dana 2012). Additionally, this unified infrastructure is more resilient in the face of certain types of natural disasters. A recent example is

Panama receiving electricity from the SIEPAC grid in May 2013 to recover from a shortage of local hydro power caused by a drought (IADB 2013). Thus, regional power generation initiatives not only allow for cost pooling among small economies in the construction of electrical systems, but also can provide benefits in terms of greater energy security and reduced electricity costs.

Regional integration efforts could also be directed at creating regional institutions and/or regulatory agencies to pool the costs of governance. Small economies often lack the resources and educated labor force necessary to maintain the government bureaucracy needed to carry out and enforce regulations. To the extent that small economies can pool resources for regulatory agencies, they can potentially increase the pool of high-quality individuals available to staff agencies. Finally, small economies can also avoid duplication of regulatory tasks among themselves, resulting in resources freed up for other uses. Such regional regulation agencies and institutions can also give small economies more power to regulate large multinational corporations in their jurisdictions, by presenting a unified front and preventing a race to the bottom in terms of relaxing or granting exemptions to regulations.

A good example of regional integration efforts in this direction is the Organisation of Eastern Caribbean States (OECS). The OECS consists of 10 Eastern Caribbean Islands and was founded in 1981 under the treaty of Basseterre. In 2010, under the revised treaty of Basseterre, the OECS became a fully unified economic area. The organization is involved in regulating and managing such diverse areas as energy markets, port regulation, and education. In some cases the OECS takes a direct role and allows the members to pool resources to address a common problem; in others, it takes a more indirect approach, allowing for the dissemination of best practices and coordination between the agencies of various member states. The OECS also conducts various export-promotion activities. It creates benefits by allowing the small island member states to act as a bloc, thus increasing their negotiating power in international agreements.

One specific example of how OECS has benefited the region relates to pharmaceutical drug procurement. Founded in 1989, the main function of the OECS Pharmaceutical Procurement Service is to negotiate drug prices at a regional level. Prior to this system, countries negotiated directly with drug companies. Drug prices varied considerably in the region, depending upon demand as well as the competence and negotiating skills of the government officers involved. When Burnett (2003) analyzed the service, he found that prices negotiated regionally for the 20 most popular drugs were 44 percent lower than individual country prices on average. This cost savings has continued, with a 7 percent reduction in drug purchase costs from 2015 to 2016 and a reduction in surcharges charged to individual governments for participation in the program (OECS 2016). In addition to these costs savings, the organization provides quality assurance standards for drugs and technical assistance to member governments, functions that might be difficult for member states to maintain individually. In sum, pooling resources and working together at the regional level have resulted in reduced costs and better outcomes in the region.

Open and Nimble • http://dx.doi.org/10.1596/978-1-4648-1042-8

In additional to regional integration efforts, small economies can consider implementing innovative systems of electronic governance. Electronic government (e-government) refers to the use of technology to provide government services and may benefit small economies, particularly small island economies, by allowing them to provide government services across great distances at lower costs. E-government can also result in increased government efficiency and better service for citizens. It is often discussed as a way to make governments more efficient and cost-effective.

In this regard, Estonia serves as a powerful example of the potential of electronic government to address problems of scale in small economies, as well as the difficulties in implementing such a system. When Estonia emerged from the Cold War, its leaders decided that, as a small country, it needed to find a niche in the global economy, and they chose to emphasize digital technology. The government supported the development of the tech sector through project Tiger Leap, an initiative aimed at providing computers and Internet access to educational institutions for research and teaching. Additionally, the government worked with the private sector to develop key technologies underlying the e-government system in use today. Namely, the government helped develop the X-rod distributed architecture, which allowed older computer systems to be integrated with new ones. This kept costs down to "between $56 and $67 million" for the whole e-government system, according to a government official (Bershidsky 2015). Today, based on the X-rod infrastructure, Estonia has an e-government system that allows for citizens to vote, file taxes, manage prescription drugs, open businesses, and access thousands of other government services online quickly and efficiently (European Commission 2016). Fostering the development of information technology industries has also resulted in a highly educated, technically savvy workforce.

The benefits of a fully functioning e-government such as that in Estonia are often framed in terms of transparency and better access to services for citizens, including increased access to information as well as increased transparency in government. The "Digital Dividends" report (World Bank 2016) notes that most people in developing countries that have a large number of electronic government initiatives use these mainly for getting information rather than interacting with the government. Additional benefits include increased transparency in government, the ability for government to receive feedback from citizens, and benefits in terms of reduced time spent dealing with the government.

A key issue in the context of small economies that has received surprisingly little discussion is whether or not e-government reduces the cost of government. Basu (2004) outlines the difficulties developing countries face in implementing e-government reform. These include infrastructure requirements (ensuring access to electricity and Internet for all) and issues with legal standards and public trust in government. He also notes that large-scale e-government may create unequal access to government services, to the extent that infrastructure is better in urban areas. In addition to these required upfront costs and regulatory changes, e-government projects have a high rate of failure, and these failures, can be extremely costly.

The World Bank's "Digital Dividends" report notes that as many as 30 percent of e-government projects are total failures abandoned before completion (World Bank 2016). Budzier and Flyvbjerg (2012) analyzed a sample of 1,355 public sector information technology projects and found that the typical project had no cost overruns and took about 24 percent more time than expected. However, Budzier and Flyvbjerg also found significant tail risk; 18 percent of projects were outliers with cost overruns greater than 25 percent.

Implementing e-government may be desirable in terms of increasing citizens' access to information, and indeed may be a necessity in the case of small island economies that face prohibitive distance costs in providing public services. However, it may not be a feasible solution for all small economies. In particular, developing small economies may not have the infrastructure and resources necessary to successfully implement effective electronic government.

Tax Reforms and FDI Policy

A greater attempt should be made at harmonizing tax codes across the region to reduce revenue losses due to tax incentives. Differing regional tax incentive structures create a "race to the bottom" dynamic as neighboring countries try to attract new sources of investment. This is particularly evident in the Caribbean. Harmonizing incentives granted to corporations seeking to invest in the region is important for maintaining consistent tax revenues. Aside from steps toward further regional integration to reduce the cost of governance and increase revenue, there are important actions countries can take individually to improve revenue generation and reduce debt burdens.

To address low levels of government revenue generation in a unilateral way, LAC governments should focus on making revenue collection more efficient and broadening the tax base, rather than simply increasing taxes. As noted by ECLAC (2006), tax rates in the Caribbean are generally fairly high already. It is unclear that simply raising rates would help raise revenue, as there are already numerous problems with enforcement. Rather, governments should focus on making the tax code more efficient and on efforts to broaden the tax base.

A frequently discussed tax-policy issue is the need to simplify the tax code and harmonize taxes across the Caribbean. Estimates by Bahl and Wallace (2007) underscore the seriousness of the problem. Their work indicates that so-called "tax expenditures" (including waivers, thresholds, incentives, and exceptions) represent as much as 61 percent of actual tax revenue collected in Jamaica. Chai and Goyal (2005) note the issue is pervasive throughout the Caribbean region, and find that incentives for companies and other tax expenditures cost eastern Caribbean countries between 9.5 percent and 16 percent of GDP per year. Further, tax incentives designed to attract FDI are not necessarily having the desired salutary effect on growth. As discussed in chapter 3, the likely problem is limited potential for FDI to develop backward linkages in small economies, with few domestic firms and a limited supply of labor beyond the workers who work for the multinational corporations (such as hotels). While fiscal incentives are not necessarily bad, it is important to maintain a rules-based approach with tax incentives rather than a discretionary one. This is especially important in small economies where aggregate public and national savings rates remain low, even when these economies should be saving, literally, for a rainy day.

Intel's investment in Costa Rica in the 1990s is an example of how a small country can successfully reap benefits from FDI and diversify its economy without giving away too much in terms of tax breaks. Spar (1998) studies the case of Intel's investment decision and notes that Costa Rica's small size initially seemed like a disadvantage when compared to its chief competitors, Brazil and Mexico. However, in the end Costa Rica won the contract by being attentive and responding quickly to Intel's needs—qualities arguably made easier by its small size (Spar 1998). Costa Rica attracted investment from Intel by offering reasonable concessions to the firm via existing export processing zone laws, which reduced some tariffs and business regulations while working closely with the company to address its specific concerns.

Crucially, Costa Rica was able to win the contract with Intel without giving the company any tax preferences beyond those offered to all foreign investors. Instead, the county worked to address Intel's business viability concerns, namely, access to an educated workforce and quality infrastructure. By working closely with Intel and addressing their actual business concerns, as opposed to simply granting additional concessions to lower their costs, Costa Rica was able to win the contract. The deal generated positive spillovers for the rest of the economy, and Costa Rica shared the costs of investment with Intel as a partner. Intel went on to make investments in Costa Rica's education system to create new worker training programs for the electronics industry, which generated positive externalities for other electronics firms. Thus, even in an extreme case where there are no spillovers generated from FDI through the channel of backward linkages, Costa Rica would still have benefited from economy-wide spillovers from these investments in education and training programs. There is also some evidence that Intel's investment acted as a signal to other technology firms, which began to invest in Costa Rica thereafter. A nascent electronics industry developed and helped diversify the export sector (Larrain, Lopez-Calva, and Rodriguez-Clare 2001).

Another important taxation issue is efficiency in revenue collection. Small economies should choose taxes that efficiently and affordably raise revenues, and should monitor the efficiency side-effects of taxes. Economists typically prescribe low taxes on international trade and FDI. The argument is that taxes on international trade such as import tariffs should be minimal, because they have two distinct distortionary effects. First, they raise the costs of imported goods for domestic consumers. Second, import taxes create incentives for domestic producers to invest capital and hire labor to produce import-competing goods that are thought to be inefficient. If domestic producers were low-cost producers, the argument goes, then import protection would not be needed. However, these arguments are much weaker for small economies. Since small economies typically do not produce many goods and services and rely on imports to satisfy domestic demand, taxes on imported goods are essentially equivalent to a national sales tax. In small economies, such a tax does not impose production-side distortions, which are a source of concern in large economies. In addition, particularly in small island economies, taxes on international trade have the added benefit of being cost-effective to administer, since they can be collected directly at the port of entry. Import tariffs thus help small countries avoid the costs of administering income taxes or other sources of tax revenues, including value-added taxes. In cases where an economy produces few products of its own and has limited resources to produce them in the future, a trade tax may function as equivalent to a sales tax.

In addition to low import tariffs, economists typically advocate low taxes on FDI. The idea is that these investments generate growth-enhancing technology spillovers and knowledge transfers to domestic firms. As previously discussed, countries in the Caribbean, and small economies more generally, have not benefited as reliably from these predicted spillover effects and backward linkages, at least in part due to their small size. Another reason to rethink FDI incentives is that foreign companies may make up a much larger share of the overall corporate tax base in smaller economies than in larger economies. Consequently, incentivizing FDI too generously could lead to a huge shrinking of the tax base, with corresponding losses in revenues. There would also be opportunity costs associated with public investments or the gains from raising national savings if the forgone tax revenues could be saved.[2]

Concluding Thoughts

The aim of this book has been to answer a relatively underexplored question: what if any impact does economic size have on economic outcomes? The core message of this book is that size does not matter for achieving high levels of economic growth. Small countries can and do grow fast and become rich.

However, a second key message is that size does have important implications that need to be taken into account when crafting policy. Small economies suffer from a lack of access to economies of scale, which does have implications for economic outcomes. They are more specialized in terms of export production, experience high levels of economic volatility, and have higher relative costs from natural disasters. Along with this, small economies also tend to have costlier governments, higher public debt, and lower savings. These are real differences in economic outcomes between small and large economies that cannot be ignored.

Aside from challenging economic conditions, small economies also have some opportunities to be exploited. They tend to be highly open in terms of trade and investment, allowing them to absorb knowledge of global best practices. They also have a remarkable degree of nimbleness and innovation in their export production. Finally, these countries send a large number of migrants abroad, who potentially represent an economic opportunity in terms of the remittance flows that these migrants send back home.

The final and perhaps most important message of this book is that there are policies to combat these economic challenges once they are recognized.

Open and Nimble • http://dx.doi.org/10.1596/978-1-4648-1042-8

Our hope is that this book can contribute to an informed discussion of the unique challenges and opportunities small economies face. Such an understanding is the first step toward achieving better development outcomes for the citizens of small economies.

Notes

1. On the issues related to accounting for contingent liabilities associated with public-private partnerships, see Engel, Fischer, and Galetovic (2014).

2. Increases in revenues would then be reflected either in declines in gross public debt (if the additional revenues are used to pay back existing debt) or in reserve accumulation if the savings are put in public savings accounts (or some sort of sovereign wealth fund), which implies a decline in net public debt.

References

Bahl, Roy, and Sally Wallace. 2007. "From Income to Consumption Tax? The Case of Jamaica." *Finanz Archiv: Public Finance Analysis* 63 (3): 396–414.

Basu, Subhajit. 2004. "E-Government and Developing Countries: An Overview." *International Review of Law Computers & Technology* 18 (1): 109–32.

Bershidsky, Leonid. 2015. "Envying Estonia's Digital Government." *Bloomberg View,* March 4.

Budzier, Alexander, and Bent Flyvbjerg. 2012. "Overspend? Late? Failure? What the Data Say about IT Project Risk in the Public Sector." In *Commonwealth Governance Handbook 2012/13: Democracy, Development, and Public Administration,* edited by Commonwealth Secretariat, 145–57. London: Commonwealth Secretariat.

Burnett, Francis. 2003. "Reducing Costs through Regional Pooled Procurement." *Essential Drugs Monitor* No. 32. World Health Organization, Geneva.

Chai, Jingqing, and Rishi Goyal. 2008. "Tax Concessions and Foreign Direct Investment in the Eastern Caribbean Currency Union." IMF Working Paper 08/257, International Monetary Fund, Washington, DC.

Charveriat, Celine. 2000. "Natural Disasters in Latin America and the Caribbean: An Overview of Risk." Working Paper 434, Inter-American Development Bank, Washington, DC.

Christensen, Laurits, and William H. Greene. 1976. "Economies of Scale in U.S. Electric Power Generation." *Journal of Political Economy* 84 (4): 655–76.

Dolezal, Adam, Anna Maria Majano, Alexander Ochs, and Ramon Palencia. 2013. "The Way Forward for Renewable Energy in Central America." World Watch Institute, Washington, DC. http://www.worldwatch.org/bookstore/publication/way-forward -renewable-energy-central-america.

ECLAC (Economic Commission for Latin America and the Caribbean). 2006. "Fiscal Policy and Tax Reform in the Caribbean." ECLAC, United Nations.

Economic Consulting Associates. 2010. "Central American Electric Interconnection System [SIEPAC] Transmission and Trading Case Study." Economic Consulting Associated Limited, London.

European Commission. 2016. "e-Government in Estonia." European Commission.

Frankel, Jeffrey. 2010. "Mauritius: African Success Story." NBER Working Paper No. 10566. National Bureau of Economic Research, Cambridge, MA.

IADB (Inter-American Development Bank). 2013. "Energy Integration in Central America: Full Steam Ahead." IADB, Washington, DC.

Larrain, Felipe, Luis F. Lopez-Calva, and Andres Rodriguez-Clare. 2001. "Intel: A Case Study of Foreign Direct Investment in Central Amesrica." In *Economic Development in Central America, Volume 1: Growth and Internationalization,* edited by Felipe Larrain et al. Cambridge, MA: Harvard University Press.

OECS (Organisation of Eastern Caribbean States). 2016. *Pharmaceutical Procurement Service Report 2016.* Castries, Saint Lucia: OECS.

Rodrik, Dani. 1998. "Why Do More Open Economies Have Bigger Governments?" *Journal of Political Economy* 106 (5): 997–1032.

Spar, Debora. 1998. "Attracting High Technology Investment: Intel's Costa Rican Plant." World Bank, Washington, DC.

Subramanian, Arvind. 2009. "The Mauritian Success Story and Its Lessons." Working Paper 2008/25, United Nations World Institute for Development and Economic Research, New York.

World Bank. 2016. "Digital Dividends." World Development Report Series. World Bank, Washington, DC.

Yepez-Garcia, Rigoberto, and Julie Dana. 2012. "Mitigating Vulnerability to High and Volatile Oil Prices." World Bank, Washington, DC.

Zafar, Ali. 2011. "Mauritius: An Economic Success Story." World Bank, Washington, DC. http://siteresources.worldbank.org/AFRICAEXT/Resources/Mauritius_success.pdf.

Distribution of Labor Force Size in Latin America and the Caribbean

As noted in the text, the choice of cutoff levels in the analysis of how economic size impacts development outcomes is a fairly arbitrary one. Here we take a closer look at how the global quartiles of working-age population used in graphs throughout this book (1.44 million, 5.3 million, and 16.36 million) divide Latin America and Caribbean (LAC) countries.

Figure A.1 presents the distribution of labor force size (in millions) across countries in Latin America and the Caribbean. Also included in the figure is an exponential trend line showing that our chosen cutoff for small of around 5.3 million (second line from the left in the figure) represents roughly the point at which the exponential growth function takes off. In fact, when looking at only countries with less than 5.3 million labor force (plus Bolivia, Haiti, and the Dominican Republic), as seen in graph B of the figure, the distribution seems more linear, suggesting 5.3 million is a fitting location for a break. An additional view of the distribution is provided in figure A.2, which shows the log difference between a country in LAC and the next smallest country in the region. Figure A.2 does not appear to provide evidence of a clear value for a break. The difference between each LAC country and the one smaller than it appears fairly random.

Figure A.1 Distribution of Labor Force in Latin America and the Caribbean in 2013

a. Distribution of the size of the labor force for LAC countries

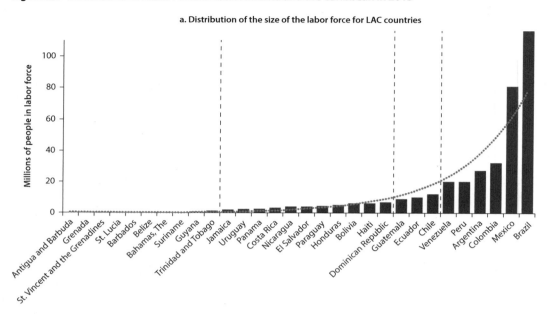

b. Distribution of the size of the labor force for small LAC countries

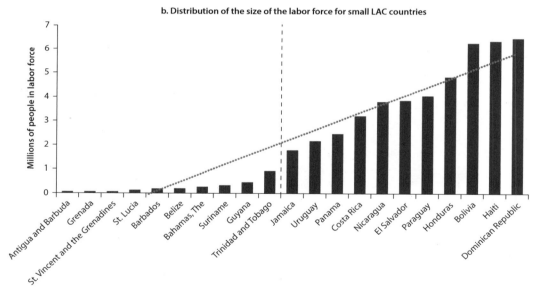

Source: Calculation based on data from World Bank World Development Indicators.
Note: Panel a shows distribution of the size of the labor force for LAC countries. The vertical lines represent, from left to right, the thresholds of 1.44 million, 5.3 million, and 16.3 million members of the working-age population. It also includes an exponential trend line. In panel b, the same figure is represented for only LAC countries classified as small, those with less than 5.3 million members of the working-age population and Bolivia, Haiti, and the Dominican Republic. Additionally, a linear trend line is added. The vertical line in panel b represents the cutoff of 1.44 million.

Figure A.2 Changes in Labor Force between Countries in Latin America and the Caribbean in 2013

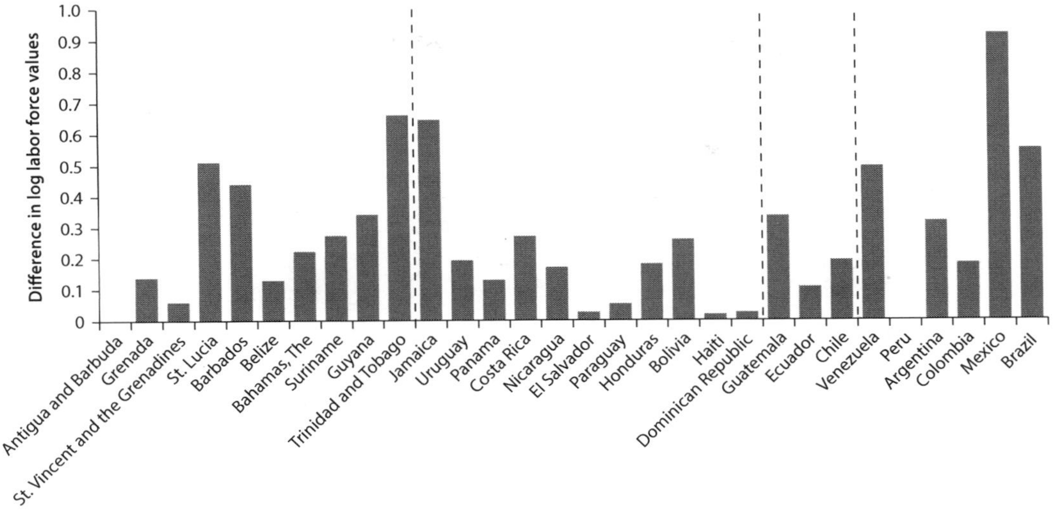

Source: Calculation based on data from World Bank World Development Indicators.
Note: The figure shows distribution of the log difference in labor force size among LAC countries. It is an approximation of the percentage change in labor force size between each LAC country and the next largest in the region by labor force size. The lines again represent the cutoffs of 1.44 million, 5.3 million, and 16.36 million labor force size used throughout this book.

Definition of Country Groups

Table A.1 Countries Grouped by Labor Force Size in 2013

Labor force grouping	Countries included in grouping
Less than 1.44 Million	Aruba; Antigua and Barbuda; Bahrain; Bahamas, The; Barbados; Belize; Bhutan; Botswana; Brunei Darussalam; Cabo Verde; Comoros; Cyprus; Djibouti; Equatorial Guinea; Estonia; Fiji; Gabon; Gambia, The; Grenada; Guinea Bissau; Guyana; Iceland; Lesotho; Luxembourg; Maldives; Malta; Mauritius; Micronesia, Fed. Sts.; Montenegro; Namibia; New Caledonia; Samoa; São Tomé and Príncipe; Seychelles; Slovenia; Solomon Islands; St. Lucia; St. Vincent and the Grenadines; Suriname; Swaziland; Timor-Leste; Tonga; Trinidad and Tobago; Vanuatu
Between 1.44 Million and 5.3 Million	Albania; Armenia; Bosnia and Herzegovina; Bulgaria; Central African Republic; Congo, Rep.; Costa Rica; Croatia; Denmark; El Salvador; Eritrea; Finland; Georgia; Honduras; Ireland; Israel; Jamaica; Jordan; Kuwait; Kyrgyz Republic; Lao PDR; Lebanon; Liberia; Libya; Lithuania; Macedonia, FYR; Mauritania; Moldova; Mongolia; New Zealand; Nicaragua; Norway; Oman; Panama; Papua New Guinea; Paraguay; Qatar; Serbia; Sierra Leone; Singapore; Slovak Republic; Somalia; Tajikistan; Togo; Turkmenistan; Uruguay

table continues next page

Table A.1 Countries Grouped by Labor Force Size in 2013 *(continued)*

Labor force grouping	Countries included in grouping
Between 5.3 Million and 16.36 Million	Afghanistan; Angola; Australia; Austria; Azerbaijan; Belarus; Belgium; Benin; Bolivia; Burkina Faso; Burundi; Cambodia; Cameroon; Chile; Côte d'Ivoire; Cuba; Czech Republic; Dominican Republic; Ecuador; Ghana; Greece; Guatemala; Guinea; Haiti; Hungary; Kazakhstan; Madagascar; Malawi; Mali; Mozambique; Netherlands; Niger; Portugal; Romania; Rwanda; Senegal; Sri Lanka; Sweden; Switzerland; Syrian Arab Republic; Tunisia; United Arab Emirates; Yemen, Rep.; Zambia; Zimbabwe
Greater than 16.36 Million	Algeria; Argentina; Bangladesh; Brazil; Canada; China; Colombia; Congo, Dem. Rep.; Egypt, Arab Rep.; Ethiopia; France; Germany; India; Indonesia; Iran, Islamic Rep.; Iraq; Italy; Japan; Kenya; Korea, Dem. People's Rep.; Korea, Rep.; Malaysia; Mexico; Morocco; Myanmar; Nepal; Nigeria; Pakistan; Peru; Philippines; Poland; Russian Federation; Saudi Arabia; South Africa; Spain; Sudan; Tanzania; Thailand; Turkey; Uganda; Ukraine; United Kingdom; United States; Uzbekistan; Venezuela, RB; Vietnam

Note: Classification based on World Bank's calculations and data from World Bank World Development Indicators Database. Labor force refers to working-age population.

Table A.2 Countries Grouped by Income Levels

Income grouping	Countries included in grouping
Low Income	Afghanistan; Benin; Burkina Faso; Burundi; Cambodia; Central African Republic; Chad; Comoros; Congo, Dem. Rep.; Eritrea; Ethiopia; Gambia, The; Guinea; Guinea-Bissau; Haiti; Korea, Dem. People's Rep.; Liberia; Madagascar; Malawi; Mali; Mozambique; Nepal; Niger; Rwanda; Sierra Leone; Somalia; South Sudan; Tanzania; Togo; Uganda
Lower Middle Income	Armenia; Bangladesh; Bhutan; Bolivia; Cabo Verde; Cameroon; Congo, Rep.; Côte d'Ivoire; Djibouti; Egypt, Arab Rep.; El Salvador; Georgia; Ghana; Guatemala; Guyana; Honduras; India; Indonesia; Kenya; Kiribati; Kyrgyz Republic; Lao PDR; Lesotho; Mauritania; Micronesia, Fed. Sts.; Moldova; Morocco; Myanmar; Nicaragua; Nigeria; Pakistan; Papua New Guinea; Philippines; Samoa; São Tomé and Príncipe; Senegal; Solomon Islands; Sri Lanka; Sudan; Swaziland; Syrian Arab Republic; Tajikistan; Timor-Leste; Ukraine; Uzbekistan; Vanuatu; Vietnam; Yemen, Rep.; Zambia
Upper Middle Income	Albania; Algeria; Angola; Azerbaijan; Belarus; Belize; Bosnia and Herzegovina; Botswana; Brazil; Bulgaria; China; Colombia; Costa Rica; Cuba; Dominica; Dominican Republic; Ecuador; Fiji; Gabon; Grenada; Iran, Islamic Rep.; Iraq; Jamaica; Jordan; Kazakhstan; Lebanon; Macedonia, FYR; Malaysia; Maldives; Marshall Islands; Mauritius; Mexico; Mongolia; Montenegro; Namibia; Palau; Panama; Paraguay; Peru; Romania; Serbia; South Africa; St. Lucia; St. Vincent and the Grenadines; Suriname; Thailand; Tonga; Tunisia; Turkey; Turkmenistan; Tuvalu
High Income non-OECD	Andorra; Antigua and Barbuda; Argentina; Aruba; Bahamas, The; Bahrain; Barbados; Brunei Darussalam; Cayman Islands; Croatia; Curacao; Cyprus; Equatorial Guinea; Faroe Islands; Greenland; Hungary; Isle of Man; Kuwait; Latvia; Liechtenstein; Lithuania; Malta; Monaco; New Caledonia; Oman; Qatar; Russian Federation; San Marino; Saudi Arabia; Seychelles; Singapore; St. Kitts and Nevis; Trinidad and Tobago; United Arab Emirates; Uruguay; Venezuela, RB
OECD	Australia; Austria; Belgium; Canada; Chile; Czech Republic; Denmark; Estonia; Finland; France; Germany; Greece; Iceland; Ireland; Israel; Italy; Japan; Korea, Rep.; Luxembourg; Netherlands; New Zealand; Norway; Poland; Portugal; Slovak Republic; Slovenia; Spain; Sweden; Switzerland; United Kingdom; United States

Note: Classification based on World Bank country income groupings as of July 2015. Low-income countries are those with gross national income (GNI) per capita less than $1,045, lower middle-income countries are those with GNI per capita above $1,045 but less than $4,125, Upper middle-income countries are those with GNI per capita between $4,125 and $12,735, and high-income countries are those with GNI per capita $12,736 or above. Figures are in US$ converted from local currency using the World Bank Atlas method.

Table A.3 LAC Countries Grouped by Region and Subregion

Region/subregion grouping	Countries included in grouping
Latin America	Argentina; Bolivia; Brazil; Chile; Colombia; Costa Rica; Ecuador; El Salvador; Guatemala; Honduras; Mexico; Nicaragua; Panama; Peru; Paraguay; Uruguay; Venezuela, RB
Caribbean	Antigua and Barbuda; Bahamas, The; Belize; Barbados; Dominica; Dominican Republic; Grenada; Guyana; Haiti; Jamaica; St. Kitts and Nevis; St. Lucia; St. Vincent and the Grenadines; Suriname; Trinidad and Tobago
Small Central American States	Costa Rica; El Salvador; Honduras; Nicaragua; Panama
Organisation of Eastern Caribbean States (OECS)	Antigua and Barbuda; Dominica; Grenada; St. Kitts and Nevis; St. Lucia; St. Vincent and the Grenadines
Small South American States	Bolivia; Paraguay; Uruguay

Table A.4 LAC Small Economies by Economic Orientation

Service oriented	Commodity oriented	Manufacturing oriented	Mixed
Antigua and Barbuda	Guyana	Costa Rica	Honduras
Bahamas, The	Paraguay	El Salvador	Nicaragua
Barbados	Suriname	Haiti	
Belize	Trinidad and Tobago		
Dominica	Uruguay		
Dominican Republic	Bolivia		
Grenada			
Jamaica			
Panama			
St. Kitts and Nevis			
St. Lucia			
St. Vincent and the Grenadines			

Note: Categories are based on shares of export in services, manufactures, and primary goods in 2014. Countries are classified in a particular category if 45 percent or more of their export value was from goods within that category. Countries classified as mixed did not have a category achieve 45 percent of total export value Trade data are from UNCTAD Stat Trade Matrices.

Variable Definitions and Data Sources

Variable	Data sources	Definition
Labor Force/Working-Age Population	World Bank, World Development Indicators Database	This variable refers to the number of people in a country age 15–64, or working age. It is calculated using the total population and the proportion of population age 15–64 from the World Development Indicators. Total population is based on the de facto definition of population, which counts all residents regardless of legal status or citizenship.
GDP per Capita PPP (2011 international $)	World Bank, World Development Indicators Database	GDP per capita based on purchasing power parity (PPP). PPP GDP is gross domestic product converted to international dollars using PPP rates. An international dollar has the same purchasing power over GDP as the U.S. dollar has in the United States. GDP at purchaser's prices is the sum of gross value added by all resident producers in the economy plus any product taxes and minus any subsidies not included in the value of the products. It is calculated without making deductions for depreciation of fabricated assets or for depletion and degradation of natural resources. Data are in constant 2011 international dollars.
Real GDP per Capita (2005 US$)	World Bank, World Development Indicators Database	GDP per capita is gross domestic product divided by midyear population. GDP is the sum of gross value added by all resident producers in the economy plus any product taxes and minus any subsidies not included in the value of the products. It is calculated without making deductions for depreciation of fabricated assets or for depletion and degradation of natural resources. Data are in constant 2005 U.S. dollars.
Trade as Percent GDP	World Bank, World Development Indicators Database	Trade is the sum of exports and imports of goods and services measured as a share of gross domestic product.
Gross Foreign Direct Investment (FDI)	World Bank, World Development Indicators Database	FDI is the net inflows of investment to acquire a lasting management interest (10 percent or more of voting stock) in an enterprise operating in an economy other than that of the investor. It is the sum of equity capital, reinvestment of earnings, other long-term capital, and short-term capital as shown in the balance of payments. This series shows net inflows (new investment inflows less disinvestment) in the reporting economy from foreign investors, and is divided by GDP.
Gross Domestic Savings as Percent of GDP	World Bank, World Development Indicators Database	Gross domestic savings are calculated as GDP less final consumption expenditure (total consumption).
Gross Capital Formation as Percent of GDP	World Bank, World Development Indicators Database	Gross capital formation (formerly gross domestic investment) consists of outlays on additions to the fixed assets of the economy plus net changes in the level of inventories. Fixed assets include land improvements (fences, ditches, drains, and so on); plant, machinery, and equipment purchases; and the construction of roads, railways, and the like, including schools, offices, hospitals, private residential dwellings, and commercial and industrial buildings. Inventories are stocks of goods held by firms to meet temporary or unexpected fluctuations in production or sales, and "work in progress." According to the 1993 System of National Accounts (SNA), net acquisitions of valuables are also considered capital formation.

table continues next page

Variable	Data sources	Definition
Percentage of Inputs of Domestic Origin	World Bank Enterprise Surveys	Represents the average percentage of inputs of domestic origin for all firms surveyed across different industries and regions within each country
Average Number of Products Exported	UN COMTRADE data for merchandise trade data. Consolidated Data on International Trade in Services v8.8 for trade in Services	Calculated using standard products in UN COMTRADE SITC1 data with 5 digits of disaggregation as well as service products at the highest disaggregation level from consolidated dataset on international trade in services. Service data go only from 1995 to 2010 while trade in merchandise data go from 1995 to 2013.
Herfindahl-Hirschman Index of Export Concentration in Products	UN COMMTRADE SITC1 for data on trade in goods Consolidated Dataset on International Trade in Services v8.8 for trade in Services	Calculated using UN COMTRADE SITC1 data disaggregated at the 5-digit level for trade in goods, and data on services from the Consolidated Data on International Trade in Services v8.8 at the most disaggregated level. Data on trade range from 1995 to 2013, while data on services range from 1995 to 2010. It is calculated for each country and year as: $\sum \left(\dfrac{X_{ji}}{X_j} \right)^2$ where X_{ji} represents the export value of product or service i from country j to the rest of the world and X_j represents overall trade from country j to the rest of the world. The results are then normalized to account for the fact that countries export different numbers of products/services.
Average Number of Export Markets	UN COMTRADE data for merchandise trade. Consolidated Data on International Trade in Services v8.8 for trade in Services	Calculated using standard products in UN COMTRADE SITC1 data with 5 digits of disaggregation as well as service products at the highest disaggregation level from Consolidated Data on International Trade in Services v8.8. Service data go only from 1995 to 2010 while trade in merchandise data go from 1995 to 2013.
Herfindahl-Hirschman Index of Export Concentration in Destination Markets	UN COMTRADE data for merchandise trade. Consolidated Data on International Trade in Services v8.8 for trade in Services	Calculated using standard products in UN COMTRADE SITC1 data with 5 digits of disaggregation as well as service products at the highest disaggregation level from consolidated dataset on international trade in services. Service data go only from 1995 to 2010, while trade in merchandise data go from 1995 to 2013. It is calculated for each country and year as: $\sum \left(\dfrac{X_{ji}}{X_j} \right)^2$ where X_{ji} represents the export value from country j to country i and X_j represents total exports from country j to the world. The results are then normalized to account for the fact that countries export to differing amounts of export markets.

table continues next page

Variable	Data sources	Definition
Terms of Trade	Penn World Table 8.1 (Feenstra, Inklaar, and Timmer 2015)	Terms of trade is calculated as (price of exports/price of imports) * 100. The indices of total import prices and total export prices available yearly in the Penn World Table were used to calculate terms of trade with the above formula.
Government Spending as Percent of GDP	IMF World Economic Outlook Database, April 2015	Total expenditure consists of total expense and the net acquisition of nonfinancial assets. Note: Apart from being on an accrual basis, total expenditure differs from the *Government Finance Statistics Manual* (GFSM) 1986 definition of total expenditure, in the sense that it also takes the disposals of nonfinancial assets into account.
Government Revenue as Percent of GDP	IMF World Economic Outlook Database, April 2015	Revenue consists of taxes, social contributions, grants receivable, and other revenue. Revenue increases government's net worth, which is the difference between its assets and liabilities (GFSM 2001, paragraph 4.20). Note: Transactions that merely change the composition of the balance sheet do not change the net worth position, for example, proceeds from sales of nonfinancial and financial assets or incurrence of liabilities.
Gross Government Debt as Percent of GDP	IMF World Economic Outlook Database, April 2015	Gross debt consists of all liabilities that require payment or payments of interest and/or principal by the debtor to the creditor at a date or dates in the future. This includes debt liabilities in the form of SDRs, currency and deposits, debt securities, loans, insurance, pensions and standardized guarantee schemes, and other accounts payable. Thus, all liabilities in the GFSM 2001 system are debt, except for equity and investment fund shares and financial derivatives and employee stock options. Debt can be valued at current market, nominal, or face values (GFSM 2001, paragraph 7.110).
Average Years of Education	Barro Lee Education Attainment Dataset	Average years of formal education attained in each country based on census data as calculated in the Barro Lee Education Database. The dataset only contains data up to 2010, we use the 2010 variable as representative of education levels in 2013.
Natural Disaster Damages	EM-DAT database	The amount of damage to property, crops, and livestock. In EM-DAT estimated damage are given in US\$ ('000). For each disaster, the registered figure corresponds to the damage value at the moment of the event, that is, the figures are shown true to the year of the event.
Number of Natural Disasters	EM-DAT database	Data on the number of disasters come from EM-DAT database. For this book we use only natural disaster data. These are defined by EM-DAT as disasters of the following type: · Geophysical · Meteorological · Hydrological · Climatological · Biological · Extraterrestrial

table continues next page

Variable	Data sources	Definition
Nominal Average Wage	International Labor Organization, Global Wage Database	Average wage data in local currency for 248 countries around the world with vary degrees of coverage from 1995 to 2011. Data are sourced mainly from local government surveys and census projects. See International Labor Organization (ILO) website for more details.
Personal Remittances as a Share of GDP	World Bank, World Development Indicators	Personal remittances comprise personal transfers and compensation of employees. Personal transfers consist of all current transfers in cash or in kind made or received by resident households to or from nonresident households. Personal transfers thus include all current transfers between resident and nonresident individuals. Compensation of employees refers to the income of border, seasonal, and other short-term workers who are employed in an economy where they are not resident and of residents employed by nonresident entities. Data are the sum of two items defined in the sixth edition of the IMF's Balance of Payments Manual: personal transfers and compensation of employees.
Labor Force Participation Rate	World Bank, World Development Indicators	Labor force participation rate is the proportion of the population ages 15–64 that is economically active: all people who supply labor for the production of goods and services during a specified period.
Unemployment Rate	World Bank, World Development Indicators Dataset	Unemployment refers to the share of labor force that is without work but available for and seeking employment. The data in the World Development Indicators are originally from country sources/surveys collected and harmonized/standardized by the International Labor Organization (ILO). Some of the observations are modeled estimates from the ILO. For this book we use the total labor force and working-age population figures from the World Development Indicators to recalculate the unemployment rate as unemployed persons/working-age population.
Emigrant Stock	United Nations Population Division	Estimates of the stock of migrants throughout the world in 2015 by country destination and origin are compiled by the UN based on population censuses. In estimating the international migrant stock, international migrants have been equated with the foreign-born population whenever this information is available, which is the case in most countries or areas. In most countries lacking data on place of birth, information on the country of citizenship of those enumerated was available, and was used as the basis for the identification of international migrants, thus effectively equating, in these cases, international migrants with foreign citizens. In this book we use the number of migrants from a given country to the world to represent the stock of emigrants abroad from that particular country.

Reference

Feenstra, Robert C., Robert Inklaar, and Marcel P. Timmer. 2015. "The Next Generation of the Penn World Table." *American Economic Review* 105 (10): 3150–82. http://www .ggdc.net/pwt.

Environmental Benefits Statement

The World Bank Group is committed to reducing its environmental footprint. In support of this commitment, we leverage electronic publishing options and print-on-demand technology, which is located in regional hubs worldwide. Together, these initiatives enable print runs to be lowered and shipping distances decreased, resulting in reduced paper consumption, chemical use, greenhouse gas emissions, and waste.

We follow the recommended standards for paper use set by the Green Press Initiative. The majority of our books are printed on Forest Stewardship Council (FSC)–certified paper, with nearly all containing 50–100 percent recycled content. The recycled fiber in our book paper is either unbleached or bleached using totally chlorine-free (TCF), processed chlorine–free (PCF), or enhanced elemental chlorine–free (EECF) processes.

More information about the Bank's environmental philosophy can be found at http://www.worldbank.org/corporateresponsibility.